It is 7 a.m. in the cardiac ward

KAMAL MALAKER

ISBN-13: 978-1724965165
ISBN-10: 1724965166

QUOTES

"Where there is love of humanity, there is also love of the art of Medicine."

Hippocrates of Kos 5th century BC

"A person starts to live when he can live outside himself."

Albert Einstein: 1879 – 1955

TO MY FATHER LATE DR MANASA CHARAN MALAKER

MY MOTHER LATE SHOROSHI MALAKER

AND

ALL MY STUDENTS AND RESIDENTS

PARTICULARLY THOSE OF ROSS UNIVERSITY SCHOOL OF MEDICINE,

DeVRY'S UNIVERSITY

AND ALL MY PATIENTS;

FROM WHOM I HAVE LEARNED MORE THAN I HAVE GIVEN THEM.

CONTENTS

ACKNOWLEDGMENT   7

Prologue   10

CHAPTER 1: Nightmare of driving along the California Coast   15

CHAPTER 2: Back at home   21

CHAPTER 3: Visiting my family physician   26

CHAPTER 4: In the cardiac ward   33

CHAPTER 5: Day 2 in cardiac ward: Eco-cardiograph experience   41

CHAPTER 6: Cardiologist's visit – my day 3 in the cardiac ward   44

CHAPTER 7: To angio-suite and back   59

CHAPTER 8: Surgeon's final thoughts, meeting with my family   71

CHAPTER 9: The lawyers and the final will   82

CHAPTER 10: What if I do not wake up?   88

CHAPTER 11: The only truth   92

CHAPTER 12: The day of preparation   102

Chapter 13: Re-operation   111

CHAPTER 14: Post-operative recovery   117

CHAPTER 15: Days in the ward   126

CHAPTER 16: Days in the ward (2)   137

CHAPTER 17: In the ward (3)   146

CHAPTER 18: Road to rehab   161

CHAPTER 19: Rehab arrangements   169

CHAPTER 20: Active physiotherapy begins   183

CHAPTER 21: Rehab and recovery   188

CHAPTER 22: Rehab program continues   195

CHAPTER 23: Return to work: a million questions   207

CHAPTER 24: Return to work: cash flow crunch   215

CHAPTER 25: Rehab continues; millions of questions; family disruption   219

CHAPTER 26: The rehabilitation: ten years down the road   223

CHAPTER 27: Learning from fellow stranger-sufferer   233

CHAPTER 28: The Epilogue   257

ACKNOWLEDGMENT

I wish to acknowledge my sincere gratitude for Dr. Bharat Shah, my family physician; Dr. Sachidananda Sinha, Cardiologist; and Dr. Edward Pascoe, Cardiac Surgeon, for their timely intervention that is allowing me today to document my experience as a cardiac patient. Also, all the Staff of the Cardiology ward of St Boniface Hospital Winnipeg, Canada for their concern, kindness and attention.

I am also grateful for the moral support from my dear wife Baljit, our darling daughter Sharmeela, our two beautiful granddaughters Princess Anaya and little Princess Aria and my son-in-law Jagdeep who kept me happy, energetic and forward looking forever. They gave me the zest for life and living.

My brother-in-law Dalip and his wife Babli's help and presence during my operative period was a huge morale booster for me and my wife being away from rest of the family. Our gratitude surpasses expression.

We are a big family and all our brothers are both successful in their chosen profession and happy at home. We thrived on each other's success and learned from our failures. This kept us together and stronger than ever. My oldest brother Amal and younger brother Nirmal are both bankers. My next brother Shyamal died in a traffic accident, his absence and the vacuum his death created is still felt and resolved us to stay even closer. Sajal (Buro) is a highly successful and popular surgeon in Bhubaneswar; another brother Utpal is a successful engineer and the youngest one Parimal (Bablu) is an internationally reputed marine engineer, but his hobby of Bengali recitation, a unique style of his own, pales the performance of professionals. He has already made a national mark.

Our oldest sister and his son Asim (Montu-babu). Our second Sister Kalyani (Kinu) are the brightest of all; they kept our homogeneity with their affection and wonderful cultural and musical talent.

My late cousin Bimal, who I was supposed to be mentoring, in death became my mentor, for me to carry on with his love for life and writing.

Outside the family, Dr. Norman Coleman of Harvard Medical School, Chairman of the Joint Center for Radiation Oncology, will ever be remembered for his kindness, his openness, forgivingness and encouragement in whatever I do, be it academic or adventurous trekking in the world's most untrodden paths. Even years after I left Boston, Norm's words of kindness still reverberate in everything I do, for pleasure or a challenging displeasure. Writing this book did not spare me of his thoughts and well wishes, in absentia.

It goes beyond just acknowledgement for Dr. Pradip Maiti and his wife Shikha for their thirty plus years of friendship and help; particularly during my grim days of illness while in and out of the hospital. Dr. Samir Bhattachariya, a colleague, and presently retired cardiac surgeon has been an intellectual partner and combatant for many years. His concern, help and active engagement with the hospital staff made my passage through surgery so much smoother and pleasant that it was beyond recognition.

Many others I should have named. My gratitude for their help and affection will forever be present in my heart as a force of inspiration.

Prologue

The last three years of my nine-year stay with Ross University School of Medicine in Dominica, I was offered an office right inside the library. When I moved in, I was impressed with the space and facilities it had—a two-room suite with all kinds of technological support right at the center of the library, yet well protected with easy access to the work station, reception and the books and journal holding areas. I wondered why the suite was not grabbed by any other senior faculty or managerial staff. I was told by the librarian that this was because it is so close to the students' area, it might be uncomfortable for the students and the faculty as well. The other most important reason was that the entire suite had no windows and they might feel claustrophobic, but those were two reasons I felt so attracted to this office suite. I cherished students' proximity during the entire working day. This period had been the most interactive time with students, staff and the library team.

When I was in the office, I always kept my office door partly open, so that anyone could knock and come in, with any question on curriculum, personal, family, neighbor at home, social, or even a friendly hello, I was always there to listen and advise if needed, like a resident faculty.

This windowless office was a boon. I had no time to gaze through the windows, looking at another part of the campus or another functional area of the campus. I could do without the distraction. The only problem was the electricity outage; having no light is livable, but without air conditioning it is murderous. Fortunately, the backup system for current outage at the campus was very efficient. During a planned outage, one would not even know of the switchover, but accidental ones might take a few extra seconds.

One day, a student knocked on my door. He had been in my office a few times before for various reasons with various questions. Today he looked particularly happy and buoyant. I thought that this was his last semester. He had done quite well both with curricular and extracurricular activities. He had all the leadership qualities and at the same time a firm determination about his career goals.

We discussed some interesting cases that he had followed with me in the hospital, during the hospital visits. He suddenly told me that he knows he will be a doctor one of these days, sooner or later, but how can he be a good doctor like me? I stared at him for a few seconds then realized he was serious and expected a serious, practical answer.

My response was, "If you want to be a good doctor, you need not be like me or for that matter anyone else; you just be yourself. All you have to do is to take off your shoes." Then I paused for a few seconds. He was kind of curious. "What does being a good doctor have to do with taking off one's shoes?" Then I said, "Put on the patient's shoes; only then will you feel and understand your patient, and that will make you a better doctor than anyone else you might have ever known."

He was a clever young man and said that he realized what I said in words was semantic only but the deeper meaning and realization was more profound.

"I am glad," I said, "that you understood the meaning behind my words."

"I guess I do, Prof! I will remember the words until I know the real meaning, but I must know how to practice. Maybe someday I will return and spend more time with you."

He left, saying good bye, because the coming weekend would be his last on the campus.

I felt sad, because I was losing a sincere and thinking young man.

For me as a teacher, I feel the best when my students leave the nest and fly away into the unknown world with confidence.

But that is not the end of my story; it is just the beginning.

After he left, I kept thinking about myself. I do think about patients, not only the illness but the impact of the illness on the patient, their family and society. I am still thinking as an observer, a third party, a news reporter and no matter how hard I try, how deep I think, I am still the third party.

A patient comes to me complaining of stomach pain, backache or even a toothache. I listen to the story of his pain; eventually one sentence comes out: "Yes! I understand what you mean." Do I really understand or I think I do? Our training teaches us to understand, even when we do not understand. We create various tools to measure a patient's agony, i.e., pain scale, nausea scale, etc. What that means to me may be nowhere close to what the patient is actually feeling, because I do not have his feelings. I am not in his shoes. But I have been in their shoes for a long time. In fact, all physicians are human and are just as likely to be sick. Unfortunately, very few of us carry the experience of being sick; the memory withers away when a patient comes to see us with a similar illness.

The student made me think, had I been sick, ever? Would the memory of the suffering of my sickness influence my judgment when I was fully recovered? Would it make me feel more deeply, more intimately about the real suffering of my patients?

This is an opportunity for me to revisit the whole process of my cardiac surgery and recovery, when I was in fact wearing the shoes of a patient. But it was at that time when I became a real doctor.

When I say to my students, my residents and my patients that you have given me more than I can ever give you, you have taught me more than I can ever dream of teaching you, I really mean that.

Let me begin the journey.

CHAPTER 1: Nightmare of driving along the California Coast

It was 7 p.m. when I began driving along the California coast in the midst of a stormy night from Los Angeles to San Diego to catch my connecting flight to Canada the next morning. It started to rain and there was a ghastly wind. The road was slippery and barely visible, with rushing traffic to my left and my right and the occasional flashing headlights from the car at my rear. Cars cutting in front of me made driving even more frightening. Driving at night on an unknown road in these most challenging conditions, I could not imagine how or when I would get to my destination more than 120 miles away.

On this dark road driving alone, I was terrified of passing cars but they kept me alert and I remained undistracted from my driving.

I was driving alone or so I thought. Suddenly a voice told me, "Keep to your lane; keep to your lane." I looked around but I could not find any backseat driver or a stowaway. It was then I realized that it was my expensive "high-tech" GPS that was talking to me. It was a wonderful, kind and loving female voice. My imagination started to fly in the clouds thinking about the voice. I checked my lane and started to wonder again about the voice. That was a dangerous distraction, considering the driving conditions back to San Diego and my return flight home.

I was focused on my driving when again I heard the voice; this time announcing, "Traffic light ahead, slow down". "Thank you, ma'am," I said. The traffic light came and went.

My ethereal companion's voice came again. "After 500 yards take a right turn; after 100 yards take the right slip road. Change to the left lane. Fifty yards to the left slip lane prepare to leave the highway. Now take the left slip road. Take the left slip road. Take the left slip road …TAKE— THE—LEFT— SLIP—ROAD." The voice was getting louder and louder, as if from a driving instructor.

The road visibility was so poor that I missed the slip road and drove straight in the darkness of the stormy night. I was very worried that I might end up in a ditch or overturn the car by the roadside.

I was wondering as I was driving on this dark, stormy and poorly visible highway, where I was having difficulty seeing anything beyond five yards ahead of me, how then my "fair lady" floating somewhere in the cloud hundreds of miles above the road could see the tiny slip road and rebuke me for not taking it as instructed.

Should I believe her or defy her? My indecision might end up with me being rear-ended and a major pile-up to follow. A frightening prospect.

Actually there was no time even to think. Somehow, someone from somewhere made me defy the instructions and follow the main road instead. I thought at least I would not end up in a ditch or overturned. Flashing headlights and fast overtaking cars, trucks and buses were all my companions for next few minutes.

It was eerily quiet inside the car for the next while. It felt like hours, not a very long few minutes. Then again the kind heavenly voice: "Recalculating; re-calculating…" It was music to my ears. Glad to be back with my companion again. "Recalculating – re– calculating."

The voice: "Fifty seven miles and three hundred nineteen yards, take left slip to turn left."

I sighed with relief, since I thought all would be quiet for a while. But that was not to be.

Again a grim, stern voice, as if an order from a newly promoted female Sergeant major, "Keep to your lane — keep to your lane."

I kept to my lane. As a matter of fact, I thought, I was already driving in my lane, where I should be.

Thanks anyway, said I, to myself.

It had already been three hours since I left Los Angeles and I was nowhere near San Diego. I blamed the unfriendly weather for this "snail craft – of driving."

For the next two hours, I drove and drove, with instructions, information and plenty of rebuke from my invisible female companion.

Almost five and a half hours of enthralling driving later, after more than an hour of silence, the lady spoke again. "We are about to reach your destination."

Then several marching orders:

-Turn right

- 69 yards take right turn

- turn right

- 25 yards take the left fork

- Slow down

- Entering the destination

- We have arrived at your destination

Then all was quiet.

The valet opened the door and the porters slowly removed my baggage to a trolley.

"Check-in is this way, sir!" said the porter.

As I looked back, I saw the car being slowly driven away.

I stopped for a second. Why did I stop? Was I expecting someone waving goodbye? Maybe. How stupid of me. Maybe the darkness of the journey had me mesmerized, fantasy became real and the feelings lingered on: no caution, no direction, and no rebuke!

Sadly! No waving hands to say goodbye.

It is 2:30 in the morning. My return flight from San Diego airport is at 7 a.m.

I checked into my room. A quick wash up and a cup of coffee in the suite, I was re-packed and ready for my next 12-hour journey home with plenty of time to sleep, ponder or perhaps dream.

Looking around at the parking lot, there was no trace of my rented car anywhere.

Maybe "the angel" is busy speaking to someone else to say, "We are 35 miles, 200 yards from our destination; it is Friday the 13th, the time is 10 pm; travelling time is one hour, 15 minutes and 41 seconds."

"For the Lord comforts his people and will have compassion on his afflicted." Isaiah 49:13

CHAPTER 2: Back at home

I returned home, mostly flying through the night from airport to airport, not sure where I was and where the flights were taking me. Eventually, the next morning at 11:00 I arrived at my home airport, took a cab and was back home in half an hour. I had just enough energy to drag my luggage inside and went straight to bed. It was not until the next evening when I was woken up by my wife, who was getting worried since I had slept for so long. She was wondering if she should call 911 or call my GP or any of our friends. She couldn't figure out if I was sick or if I was just tired. It is very unlike me to sleep for over 24 hours.

It must have been the stressful drive through the night from LA to San Diego in very unfriendly weather and driving with unfriendly traffic. Hopping from airport to airport to reach my city in Canada, which normally should take four hours instead took just over 24 hours, due to the scheduling genius of the modern American air traffic system.

On my arrival home the next day at about 12 noon, I did not realize how tired I was. I sat on the sofa and slept until it was 8 p.m. My wife let me have my way for a change; she realized how tired I was and did not want to interrupt my well-earned restful sleep, despite how uncomfortable it looked to her.

I woke up fresh, full of vigor and told her the whole saga of my trip from LA to home. I had a light dinner, looked at my laptop and the desktop at home, hoping to discover something unusual and exciting, instead of all the routine stuff including clever salespersons' intellectual pitch to drag me into their circle at 20% discount if I purchase, subscribe or introduce a friend within the next 24 hours. Fascinating. There are "quick buckers" all over; without even moving a finger one wants to become a millionaire. Some also call them "entrepreneurs", an excellent façade for many of them. Thanks to modern technology, thanks to 'www.', thanks to the Internet.

With these amusing thoughts I went to bed again and fell asleep unnoticed.

Suddenly, in the middle of the night, around 2:30 a.m., I woke up with slight nausea and much acidity. I have never suffered from acidity before, never. I thought it must be the stress of the travel, untimely eating and sleeping in odd places, with even odder beds and supports.

I went down to the kitchen, had a glass of ice water and returned to bed. I woke up in the morning, not with my usual freshness, but awake and ready to go. Where? I just came home for few days of rest before I started my new assignment in South America. The day went well, with friends dropping by, calls from abroad, my siblings and my in-laws, my old colleagues and classmates, etc. The day went well; with socializing, advising, chatting and of course daydreaming, some of my favorite pastime.

During the middle of the night, I woke up again with severe acidity, heartburn and nausea. Again, the kitchen came to my rescue. I popped a couple of antacids and drank ice water. The discomfort eased off greatly but did not go away completely. I went to sleep. The same thing happened on the third night. I thought I must have caught the same virus that my wife had, which did give similar symptoms, just before I came. I thought to myself that I had an answer.

On the fourth night the heart burn was much more severe. I actually vomited, had giddiness and my pulse was running high. But I did not have a fever, in spite of feeling cold and having chills.

With a relatively rough night, I woke up in the morning feeling miserable and told my wife, "I do not think it is your flu, that I caught, but maybe something else. I will go to check with my family physician."

He was happy to hear my voice and said, "Come immediately, let me check you up. Then we can decide which way to go."

I was wondering if it was worth it to hassle a busy family physician, just for the heartburn I had for the last four days, which would not go away. I thought to myself, I could have tried medication and dietary adjustment for a few more days, and if it still persisted then go to see him. On the other hand, I said to myself, I have tried all possible antacids, restricting my diet to "palatably spicy" food—and I am addicted to a "high spice index"—and all seems to have eluded me. It could even be "acid reflux", which is so common nowadays, once one understands in the early phase it can be reversed. I started to convince myself, most likely that was what it was, and exercise, dietary change and perhaps unorthodox practices like yoga and meditation could cure my severe heartburn, which I had started to convince myself was nothing but an early case of acid reflux which can be reversed.

However, many other more sinister conditions which can give severe heartburn include acid-producing tumors of the stomach, serious diseases of the pancreas, gall bladder and liver problems; even the possibility of a heart attack flashed through my mind, which I ignored. I remembered in the medical school, professors teaching us gave us this "mantra": while investigating a patient, think of "common things first" and keep the rare condition in the 'appendix' chapter of your mind. That is what I have done throughout my medical teaching career. In this case I may be the patient but, why should I not practice what I teach?

So the simple things first. With that conviction, I set out to see my family physician, who also happens to be a friend.

In whom there is no sympathy for living being know him as an outcast
-The Sutta Nipata.

CHAPTER 3: Visiting my family physician

Just a short time later, the doctor came to me and asked me to come with him to his examination room. It was a neat, clean and smartly designed clinic. After chatting with each other about our families and the local medical fraternity he suddenly said, "You are travelling too much. You look very tired and exhausted. When did you return from your trip?"

"Five days ago," I said.

"Oh! In that case you had enough time to recover. I hope the last five days of rest had some impact, but you still look very exhausted. Unless you are having one of those flus, for which we, the medical community, have very little to offer, just reassurance, drink plenty of water, maintain your daily physical activities, and any painkiller that suits you. Take plenty of rest as well and keep mentally busy. Etc., etc. I hope that is what you have. Let me examine you, if you do not mind."

"It is a waste of your time," I said. "It is minor indigestion only, but it certainly made me very tired, mind you, I had interrupted sleep for last four nights or so."

Anyway, he examined me thoroughly. I had never before seen him so thorough for just a physical examination.

He kept counting my pulse and feeling it as well. As he started to examine me and listened to my chest and my heart, his face got grimmer and grimmer by each turn of his stethoscope.

In the end he said, "Kamal, I will drive you to another doctor, who should be able to better determine that there is nothing really wrong with you. Sorry! I forgot to tell you that we are going to see our friend the cardiologist so he can examine you."

A cardiologist—why a cardiologist? I have no problem with my heart. No chest pain, no shortness of breath; I do climb up and down the stairs in my house several times a day. I do not have high blood pressure, nor do I have any kidney problems. I was never a smoker. I smoked only as a student in medical school, to gloss over my "macho" image as a student leader and impress the girls in the college. Aside from being girls, they were my ardent supporters in student politics and very precious indeed. That was several decades ago.

As I listened to my family physician talking about consulting a cardiologist, I inadvertently, without realizing what I was doing, started to check my own pulse— a habit perhaps. When anyone needs medical help and goes to a doctor or health care person, one of the rituals is to check the patient's pulse. It is not necessarily a ritual, but an essential part of examining the patient's condition. This also causes a bond between the patient and the doctor, a reflection of the doctor's concern and level of expertise as perceived by the patient. How often a doctor checks a patient's pulse by himself usually depends on the pulse-meter, the nurse or medical assistant's interpretation. The human touch and expression of empathy is sorely missing.

Regardless, I could not identify my pulse and gave up in the end. I followed my GP, who drove me to see the cardiologist. We arrived at the hospital, where the cardiologist and his team were ready for me. After a very short time dealing with the bureaucracy, checking my "health card", I was chaperoned straight to the cardiology "Clinical Lab" where the cardiologist was waiting. He directed me straight to an examination couch. He examined me from head to toe. I must admit perhaps because of his specialty or being a professional colleague, he took my blood pressure and checked my pulse with his fingers himself, in spite of the young doctors, medical students, and nurses being in attendance.

He himself did my cardiograph or EKG as the medical term goes, sent blood for testing to the lab and so on. Until this point, I had no idea why I was wasting the time of such a busy cardiologist of our city. I still had no symptoms I could directly link to heart problems, although it is well known, there are "fifty shades of heart attack".

Next, I was asked to go on a treadmill. I did.

The machine started to roll on. The cardiologist was watching; the technician was telling me that she was increasing the speed. Later she said, "I am raising the height." She kept looking at the monitor and kept asking me, "Are you all right? Can we go one speed higher?" Then we raised one notch higher.

"Yes, you can," I said.

"OK," she said.

The treadmill was rolling fast and at the same time slowly, very slowly going up. I thought I was getting some shortness of breath, feeling giddy, pain in my chest. My thoughts were getting cloudy. I thought my speech was beginning to sound funny.

I told the technician how I felt.

"You are doing very well; just a little more, and you will hit the normal," the technician said.

I could not hear her anymore; I think I did collapse on the treadmill. I have no recollection of the event. I failed to hit the normal, I guess, and disappointed the technician. When I became aware, I found myself on the examination bed. A drip of some sort was being infused into my vein. My cardiologist was removing the ECG terminals from my chest one by one.

"You just blacked out for a couple of seconds. Nothing to worry about! It does happen on the 'mill'. Now we know your limits, which are not very far from normal. That is what I was expecting."

There were quite a number of people around. I realized the cardiologist did not take any chances and had summoned the Cardio-Pulmonary Resuscitation (CPR) team. As I started to speak the CPR team quietly left.

The cardiologist then said, "I just got your cardiac enzyme and chemistry level. It is very high. I have to keep you in the hospital. We will do a few more tests and find out how healthy you are concerning your heart."

I still kept wondering how come I had no symptoms of heart disease but my enzymes were raised. I kept pondering but did not want to harass my friend.

Then the wheelchair took me to the ER reception, where my papers for admission would be processed. There were at least fifty very anxious people, some in much discomfort, waiting in the waiting room. The area was crowded. Some of them were not patients but were worried relatives or friends. My wheelchair went past them to the reception. As soon as I arrived, the receptionist gave all my admission papers to the nurse who was wheeling me around. I did look at the faces of several people in agony waiting for their turn. I felt rather embarrassed for 'jumping the queue'. The receptionist looked at me and said, "It is alright Dr.; she will take you to the cardiac ward." As I entered the cardiac ward an elderly lady greeted me and escorted me to my assigned room. A bed had already been prepared awaiting my arrival.

Slowly I settled on the bed in my hospital room. But every now and then, the pale faces, the anxious looks and the apparent physical discomfort of some flashed through my mind. Some were breathing hard, some were clutching their hands and others were dozing or half asleep on the not so comfortable chairs or on the shoulder of their relative or company on the way in and out of the Emergency Department's waiting area.

I kept thinking perhaps I did not get the real story from my doctors. I must be really very sick, which I can't perceive or do not want to believe. Or I was really one of the privileged ones to receive such wonderful and caring attention. The faces I left behind in the emergency room kept flashing back for the next couple of days. I could not help it.

By this time my GP had left and my wife arrived to find out what was happening. She also had no idea why I was being admitted to the cardiac ward since I had gone to see my GP for indigestion. She was confused and quietly asked me, "What's wrong with your heart?" She had not lost her sense of humor, though scared, and said, "I hope they do not poke your heart instead of your stomach."

I told her that the cardiologist is our friend, highly respected and admired for his professional competence and academic contribution. I am sure he will poke my heart instead of stomach, if that is what is needed.

She was perplexed but uneasily reassured. She kept wondering what was actually wrong with me.

CHAPTER 4: In the cardiac ward

I was still in a kind of daze when I was wheeled into the cardiac ward but alert to what was happening around me. The nurse brought me to a room with two beds. It is safer to be with another patient, unless one has a 24-hour attendant to monitor. In the cardiac ward in this hospital, one does not need an attendant. All monitoring is done remotely, which I will elaborate on later.

I had to remove my clothes and change into the hospital gear that was given to me. Everything I had in my possession — my wallet, watch and clothing — except my glasses was bundled in a bag, sealed and labeled. It was removed by a senior nurse for safekeeping, which I would need when I was discharged home.

I was put to bed and tucked in by a nurse, apparently a student nurse, as part of her practical training. She weighed me, measured my height, took my pulse, my blood pressure, temperature and charted it all. A few minutes later another lady entered.

"Good afternoon Doctor, I hope you are feeling better," she said and went over all the figures the young nurse had charted. I could see she was the ward sister in charge; the name label was clearly written on her ID badge. She checked my pulse and blood pressure again and seemed to have agreed with the young student nurse.

"The resident-on-call will be here shortly to admit you and check you through, before we inform the senior cardiologist under whom you have been admitted to come and see you."

Soon a young lady with white lab coat entered and introduced herself as Dr. Geremy Joules. She was the chief resident of the cardiology program and asked if she could examine me to report to the cardiologist.

Before the young Doctor even completed her examination, our friend the cardiologist who examined me in the outpatient clinic appeared and arranged for admission and said, "I would like to carry out further tests."

He told me that one critical blood test that he did just after I collapsed in the clinic, was very high, four to four and a half times more than an average healthy man of my size, age and lifestyle. He also said the test will be repeated again and further decisions will be made on the basis of the new result. He reassured me and my wife that no plans had yet been made and that I might be allowed to go home tomorrow or might stay longer after all the tests had been carried out.

The young doctor spent several minutes discussing with the cardiologist and returned to complete her examination documenting those in my file. Before she departed, she said, "We have to do several other tests. As soon as we receive the report of your second blood test, maybe within the next couple of hours, I will come and discuss all the tests the cardiologist is anticipating may have to be done. Whatever is needed we will start arranging them from tomorrow. Some of the blood tests need to be done before breakfast. Either the ward sister or I will confirm later this evening."

In the meantime, I had several injections, some tablets and by the evening I was full of energy. All my symptoms of heartburn, tiredness, headache, and giddiness that I experienced in the cardiology clinic had disappeared. I felt rested and hopeful, imagining that the result of my second blood test will come back as normal and I would be discharged home tomorrow, as the cardiologist indicated.

But I kept an open mind, hoping to hear from the young doctor or the sister-in-charge, about what came next.

The dinner came at 6 p.m. I have never tasted hospital food but seen it umpteen times. I hardly remember consciously taking the lid off to inspect what was underneath the cover. We talk about the diet; advise, discuss, dissect and degrade, but never ever volunteer to taste what our patients are eating, while they are healing in the hospital. Dieticians and nutritionists are all determined and eager to speak to doctors, but I wonder how often practicing doctors focus seriously on their patient's diet offered in the hospital.

The diets are scientifically aggregated, calorie counted, fat, protein, carbs and micro-nutrients balanced and served hygienically timely on a physiological rhythm. But how often are patients asked if they are hungry or if they like the food served?

I wonder.

Now it is my real time to do all those things which we missed to learn in medical schools and failed to integrate into our clinical practice.

I looked at the tray — a well-balanced composition, clean, well-served, but uninviting for my palate. It would be a great shame and insult to the dietetics and catering team, if I did not make some effort to consume some of their offerings. I did and I forgot immediately what I did in three seconds. My body was full but my soul remained empty; my real hunger thrived, only to be dampened by a fistful of tablets I was consuming every day, throughout the day.

Such was the impact of my first encounter with the hospital diet.

Nonetheless, they are healthy and nutritious.

By this time, I was surrounded by my friends, colleagues, students and my wife. Being a stable and active member of the community and my workplace for decades, there were as many friends and that many foes. But at the time of crisis, as it is now, prayers were recited from both sides, for different or completely opposite reasons. Prayers are prayers, aiming for heaven for the grace of God to fulfill wishes; good or bad is not important.

Everybody was relieved to see me not in tubes and hanging bags, monitors of different kind for different purposes hanging in the wall or outside. Someone even joked that "it is nice to see a healthy fraud than a battered one."

Slowly my visitors left one by one except my wife, who left last.

Although I felt well, the gloom of tiredness and somnolence did not quit completely.

By 8:30 in the evening, a young boy who appeared to be from South East Asia, most likely the Philippines appeared with his trolley full of 'things'. "Sir," he said, "we have instructions from the senior cardiology staff to send blood for few more tests. If you do not mind I will take the blood samples. It is just one quick prick and will be over in a couple of minutes." The Filipinos have made enormous contributions to the running of health services in the entire Western world, particularly in the nursing profession, especially the English speaking one.

He followed the "Pre-puncture rituals" and was ready to prick. It was not my imagination but I thought I saw his hands shaking. First prick - no blood; second prick the same. I suggested that perhaps he would like to try the other arm.

He said, "I would like to give another try in this arm." This time blood came shooting from the site of the 'prick'. I thought we were in an artery rather than in a vein, looking at the force of the spurt. He kept pressure on the bleeding site for nearly eight minutes before it stopped oozing. There was a hematoma in the front of my right elbow.

I reassured him and said, "Not to worry, this can happen to anyone even with lots of experience."

He said, "I will call the night sister to help me to take a blood sample before I destroy all possible sites." A very honest and daring admission from a young nurse.

His hands were still trembling, his face was flushed and an air of distress and embarrassment could easily be spotted on his face and body in general.

He took all his possessions and retreated to the nearby preparation room.

The night sister entered. She apologized for the incident and said, "The young Filipino nurse is very efficient and good at work. The fact that he came to know that you are a doctor and a senior specialist, established in the profession and the community, also noting your visitors, that you had several from this institute, made him nervous."

I did reassure him not to get upset.

Sister's one tourniquet, one tap and one prick on the back of my forearm, there came seven samples of my blood for various tests as the doctor ordered done. No hassle, no fuss, a peak of expertise and professionalism.

I thanked her. She left saying, "I will be around the rest of the night should you need any help, please press this red button. I hope you have a restful night." She departed.

After a little while, just after 9 p.m., the Senior Cardiologist appeared in my room. I was surprised to see him. Casually, he said, "I am glad that you are not asleep. I would have hated to wake you up. I thought I should tell you about our next plan of action. Unfortunately two follow-up tests of your cardiac enzymes, that is, Troponin are consistently high; if anything it is rising very slowly. Although the level of rise is still within the acceptable margin of error, I thought we need to do all the required tests to determine the state of health of your heart and then determine if we need further help to bring it to normal. I came this late, because tomorrow morning they have scheduled your heart test at 7 a.m., which is called 'eco-cardiogram'. It is to determine the functioning state of your heart. As you know, it is just an ultra-sonic scan and there is no risk involved in the procedure. In the morning, when I come to visit you, the result and report will be ready so that we can plan further ahead. Good night, sir," said the cardiologist, who is a colleague and also a friend. He departed, tired and pensive. The courtesy was over-expressed, I thought.

"Compassion and tolerance are not a sign of weakness but a sign of strength."   - Dalai Lama

CHAPTER 5: Day 2 in cardiac ward: Eco-cardiograph experience

At 6:30 a.m., someone woke me up the next morning and suggested that perhaps I would like to go to the washroom for brushing my teeth, washing my face and getting ready to go for my eco-cardiograph.

I did exactly as I was requested. I then changed to a hospital gown from my night sleeping suit. One orderly put me on a stretcher and slowly rolled out of the room.

I asked him, "Why on the stretcher? As I am feeling now I can easily walk or be on a wheelchair, instead of this stretcher."

The orderly said, "We have instructions to transport you on stretchers; unless stated otherwise we can't use any other form of transport."

We arrived at the eco-cardiogram department where the receptionist greeted me. A nurse checked my vitals and then a technician chaperoned me to the eco-cardiogram room, where the test would be carried out.

Soon enough another lady entered with her white coat on. She introduced herself as Dr. Sharon King, the staff imaging physician, who would give the report to my cardiologist.

She explained the procedure and emphasized that there would be no anesthesia, no injection or medication needed to do the procedure. The technician would perform the scanning, while she would monitor the images and the technique from her office just across this room on the other side of the corridor. She also showed me a flashlight-like gadget, which would be used to do the scan.

I was already wearing a hospital gown with the front open. The technician helped me to go up onto the couch where the test would be carried out. The technician put some jelly on my chest and on the left side over my heart and started maneuvering it from side to side, from above downward. The technician showed me the overhanging monitor screen, where I could see my heart pumping, bare like bones but hard at work.

After about an hour, the technician said, "I am done with the procedure. I will let Dr. King know and she will speak to you about the rest." Dr. King entered and explained that the procedure had been completed satisfactorily and she hoped it did not cause any discomfort. She informed us that she would send the report to the cardiologist soon.

The nurse again helped me to get off the examination table and rolled over to the stretcher. The procedure is completely free from any discomfort except the application of the jelly as a conducting agent.

She wished me well and handed me over to the ward assistant to wheel me back to the ward. By 8:30 a.m. I was back in the ward and ready for my delayed breakfast.

"Healing comes from taking the responsibility to realize that it is you and no one else that creates your thought and action."
                                                              - Peter Shepherd.

CHAPTER 6: Cardiologist' s visit – my day 3 in the cardiac ward

It is routine every day that at around 10 a.m., the cardiologist visits all the patients admitted under him in the unit with his entourage. For me it is 'not routine' – my day 3 in the cardiac ward. After the eco-cardiogram and all the blood and urine tests I had yesterday, the results will be reviewed, analyzed and a plan of action will be determined. That is what the Chief Resident of the unit, who came about half an hour prior, told me. He had a quick enquiry about me and the experience about the Eco-cardiogram procedure, etc., and mentioned that they were expecting the cardiologist to come any time now.

Indeed he entered right on time with his chief resident and the ward sister-in-charge. "Good morning," he said and asked if I had a good night's sleep and felt rested.

"Yes!" I said. I had a young roommate, who was admitted in the second bed in my room. Unfortunately, he was not there during the cardiologist's visit, having left; either discharged or transferred to another ward.

There were lots of murmurs, machines on wheels in and out of the room, some people in lab coats and some in scrub suits.

That is all I remember, I dozed off soon after and rested for the rest of the night.

I did not have to tell the story to my cardiologist friend. I said, "Yes, indeed! I had a restful night and I feel very well. I feel like I can go back to work."

The specialist smiled and said, "Your eco-cardiogram is good and informative, so now we can plan what next."

"What is next?" I asked.

"Now we need to carry out a couple of more tests to make a final decision. I am arranging for an angiography, which you know will be done through cardiac catheterization, and also a MUGA scan. The MUGA scan is a test similar to eco-cardiography, but we use radioactive isotopes to study the heart. The information we find is complimentary to the eco-cardiography and enables us to understand the state of your heart better, so that we can plan what to do and what not to do."

It is interesting to hear from the cardiologist, explaining to me about the MUGA scan and the process of Cardiac catheterization, which I had been explaining to my patients whenever the tests are needed for them.

Now it is my turn to understand and go through the process, as advised to me. Strangely enough I had no questions to ask the cardiologist, who said, "The Interventional radiologist will see you shortly and explain the process and if it is possible, I will ask him to do it tomorrow, if he can fit you in." Of course I knew about Interventional radiologists and the kind of specialists they are. I spared him answering questions, which he might have done for other patients.

He checked my heart, looked at the last ECG pictures and said that I would be put on continuous monitoring.

Again! I stopped myself asking, 'Why continuous monitoring? Am I at real risk of some serious events? What are you monitoring?' Instead I let him carry on with his plan of action for me.

As soon as he left, the resident doctor came with another young lady. She had some button-like things in her hand. She said, "The specialist instructed us to put you on continuous CVP (Cardio-vascular-pulmonary) monitoring. I have a few little buttons which I am going to place on your chest and sides with some adhesive to retain them in place. These are electronic transmitters, which will continuously send data of your heart, blood pressure, respiration, serum oxygen saturation, and carbon dioxide and nitric oxide level to a receiver outside your room, connected to a monitor. The data will be recorded 'live', which is being watched by the staff in the nursing station. There is also a warning system which produces sounds in case any of the data recordings become critical. The medical staff will be alerted by the alarming sound to give you immediate attention."

She also said, "It is not only the critical data that warns the staff; it also warns of any mechanical malfunction, any problem with the transmitter or receiver or the Internet wireless system that conveys the information."

I have seen these monitors outside patients' rooms in the Intensive care unit, in the ER, but had very little understanding of the process that takes place to make it work. This is no doubt a marvel of modern science that is helping to save many lives by timely intervention.

I had about twelve 'button-like pieces' taped on my body, mostly on the left side of the chest and some also near my ankle. Later another man came who informed me that he is an electronic engineer from the IT department and that he came to check the connectivity. He was happy and left with some degree of satisfaction.

The cardiologist advised that the invasive imaging specialist would be coming to see me and indeed he did. He arrived at 2 p.m. and introduced himself as Dr. Morey Levitt, a smart, well-attired, well-spoken, sprightly, polite and respectful young man. He graduated from this medical school, had specialist training in McGill University in Montreal, Canada, John Hopkins school of medicine in Baltimore, USA and joined this hospital, about two and a half years ago. He had a wonderful time here and hopefully it would be forever.

The radiologist said, "Sir! I know I do not need to explain the procedure because you know all about it but I must for legal and bureaucratic reasons. I will be as short and as precise I can."

I said, "There is always something to learn. Please take your time and explain just as you would to any other patient. You never know what I might learn from you. After all I am the patient, my perception as a doctor may be different from what a patient might perceive. Please go ahead."

Dr. Levitt took a deep breath and said, "I do remember you as staff during my medical school days here."

I said, "That helps; I am reassured. I can't be in any better hands. Thank you."

He explained that to carry out the procedure, he would give me a short-acting intravenous general anesthesia just to perform the procedure. As soon as it was done, I would be wide awake without experiencing any pain or discomfort or lasting side effects.

To do the actual procedure, he would make a short incision in my right groin to expose the artery through which he would introduce a special fine catheter which are fine plastic or silicon tube would be pushed upward into the heart. This had special kinks to conform to the curvatures of the big artery. As he pushed the catheter, he would be squirting some white dyes, which would show the interior of the arteries and that of the heart in the monitor which he would be watching to direct the catheter toward my heart.

If there was any narrowing, he said that he would try to dilate the narrowed part with a balloon or retain a stent which would keep the opening of the narrowed part.

"Well, I hope it is all clear to you. I will try to schedule your procedure as the first case which starts at 7 a.m. Just like any surgical procedure you need to have a light meal for dinner and not to eat or drink after midnight. Please expect a visit from an anesthetist this afternoon. You need to sign the consent form for the procedure if it is OK with you."

I quickly scanned the consent form, put my signature on it and handed it to him.

"Thank you, sir. I will see you tomorrow." He departed.

Soon after, the anesthetist arrived. He asked me about my allergies, medications if any, any surgeries and if I had any reason to have general anesthesia before. He explained that in my case anesthesia, a medication will be given intravenously to make me fall into deep sleep. "There will be no lasting effect; you will be almost fully awake as soon as we stop infusing the medication."

I had a reasonable idea about the procedure. I have watched several. It felt very safe and mentally attuned for the procedure.

The difference is as I watch patients being put to sleep, I am fully aware of what is going on in their body, watching their movements and looking at the monitor, I feel "In control". But when I am anesthetized, I will not be there to watch "me" nor the monitor giving my physiological info. Suddenly I felt insecure "out of control", but woke up soon enough to be realistic to refrain from any unnecessary anxiety.

The anesthetist checked my heart and lungs again, then checked all the investigations carried out and then asked that I sign the consent form for anesthesia. This is mainly for the protection of the institute and performers. In this 'legislative world' who knows how the simplest issue can get twisted out of control to an unimaginable level.

The anesthetist left after leaving instructions written in my chart for next morning's procedure.

I feel that I am all set for the coronary angiogram. In the back of my mind is always one question: what actually is wrong with me? Is it my heart or something else? I may have a problem with my heart and at the same time, the stomach issue may be a real one and my heart is overshadowing the stomach. I promised myself that I will bring it up to my cardiologist and ask him to consider it; although at present I neither have any problem with my heart nor with my stomach.

I can't understand why all these uncertainties and irrational thoughts are overhanging my rational and scientific mind. I opened a book called "History of Russia, the beginning" and tried to concentrate on events far away from what was happening now with me.

I am all set for coronary Angiogram tomorrow at 7 a.m. I will be the first patient on their list.

At around 3:30 p.m., Dr. Davis from the department of nuclear medicine visited me. It was about the MUGA scan. My cardiologist apparently personally requested the department to do the test as soon as possible. She repeated the technique as my cardiologist explained earlier, the procedure and the use of a very minute quantity of radioactive chemical to perform the test. Totally harmless and there is no immediate or late onset of side effect for its use.

I was well aware of the test and the use of radioactive chemicals, so I spared her going through the details of the test, risks and benefits etc.

In the end she said, the test would be done the day after tomorrow since I was going to have my coronary angiogram tomorrow. I needed to sign another consent form for the use of radioactive substance for the test.

The bureaucracy of health care is fascinating. It gets more interesting as one gets involved as a user, not as a provider. My eyes were opening as I lay in my hospital bed thinking of the monstrous bureaucracy we have created to deliver the care, the weight of which is overbearing and unbearable by the system of 'Care' which might collapse into pieces any time. On the other hand, the 'system of care' may be too strong for the bureaucracy to make a dent in it because of the resilience of individuals involved in providing health care.

Anyway, let me get ready for tomorrow and the day after tomorrow and the day after, until I am fit to go home.

I started to introspect. I know everybody is doing their best, doing the right thing, very kind, respectful and courteous; in that case why I am feeling resentful? There is absolutely no reason for this. Depressed? Depressed at being sick or depressed at abusing the system?

None of the above. Just not knowing what is wrong. I had no clear answer for my patients many times in my several decades of practice. The feeling is clear now.

By 5 p.m. the room is filled with friends, colleagues and well-wishers from the community. Several others had to wait in the lobby, until some visitors left to make room for others. I was more than overwhelmed by the sympathy and well wishes showered onto me for my quick recovery.

By 6 p.m., the room had to be cleared, since dinner was to be served. My wife brought some home cooked items, which I consumed with relish. When the ward aide came to collect the tray, she noticed that I had not touched any items at all. I told her that my wife brought my dinner from home and although

I did like the hospital food, I have a small capacity stomach to consume two dinners in one go.

"I had enough to eat; you may report to your superior that there is nothing wrong with the food, only I had another choice which I opted for. Please extend my greetings to the Chef and the kitchen staff for their excellent attention."

As the evening rolled on, I felt tired and eventually fell asleep around 10 pm.

Around 2 p.m. I woke up with lots of noise and many people surrounding the second bed. Another patient was admitted through ER department with an alleged heart attack. In the ER, if the tests and examinations showed a massive heart attack, the patient is supposed to be admitted to ICU, but due to lack of available beds in the A&E department, he was sent to the ward and put in my room.

Everybody around him was the hospital staff since all relatives were asked to wait in the waiting room. The elderly gentleman soon became unconscious and the Code Blue team was summoned. The old man appeared dead despite all the efforts from the Code Blue team to bring him back to life. Or so I thought.

A very sad night. I have watched many deaths, certified many deaths and helped to revive patients, sometimes with success and other times failure. But it is a strange feeling, when I am in the same room where my roommate may have died on the bed next to me, no matter how short a time we were sharing that room. Me as an onlooker, helplessly biting my nails off; now, he is perhaps dead and I am still kicking on the next bed in the same room.

From time to time staff from the nursing station came running to me asking if I am ok. They checked my vitals a few times, while the resuscitation team was working on my new roommate. Later, they told me that they had been watching the monitor which was receiving data transmitted by the small transmitter attached to my skin. They received live information in the monitor with warning sounds from time to time in last hour or so, they said.

These warnings are most likely what was going in my room on the next bed which affected me both mentally and physically, the response was eventually transmitted to the monitors. Sometimes, my heart pumped faster, my pulse was feeble, at times my breathing was labored, blood oxygen level fluctuated, and all these changes were remotely monitored at the nursing station. Luckily, my room was just next to the nursing station, within their direct watch. I was well medicated not to have any whimsical behavior by my heart and lungs. Yet I did. Fortunately I did not feel anything. My attention was more focused on what was happening to the person on the next bed.

I was impressed with the attention the nursing staff gave me in spite of another patient with an acute medical condition in the same room. Fortunately, the 'Code Blue' team was able to make him breathe on his own and the heart started to pump again without any aid. I could see the monitors attached to him were all going full speed, staggering maybe but still going nevertheless. They brought him back to this world again to his family and friends.

Slowly the team left; the lights in the room were dimmed and his bed was re-organized. I guess someone from his family was allowed to sit beside him but I could not see the face well in the dim light of the room. But I could imagine how it might be.

I dozed off, exhausted both physically and mentally, by 2:30 a.m.

I was woken up by a heavy-built man. "Good morning, Doc!" he said. "It is nearly 7 a.m. Your angiography is scheduled at

7:15. You can have your breakfast after the test. Perhaps you would like to brush your teeth and be fresh. These are your tablets you need to take them now, before you go to the 'Angio-suite'. The orderly from Angio will come to take you on a stretcher there. By the way, I am Nurse Thompson. I hope you were able to catch up on some sleep last night." Then he departed.

He reminded me about last night. I looked left. The room was empty. There was no bed, no patient; even the anxious relative was not there. The curtains were pulled aside and the other half of the room appeared to have been deserted. I said to myself, 'Maybe they have wheeled him for some tests to another part of the hospital. But why is the bed not there? Why was his side table clean?' It did not make any sense.

A short while later the orderly arrived, along with Nurse Thompson. I was transferred from my bed onto the stretcher without getting up. These guys were experts. As we were leaving the room, I asked Nurse Thompson, "What happened to the patient who was admitted in my room last night?"

He said, "Unfortunately he suffered another heart attack soon after the Code Blue team left. They returned and tried hard to revive him. Even before he could be transferred to the cardiac

ICU unit he passed away in his bed. He was only 69 years old."

I was not expecting this answer from him. That is the reality. I was unable to think; I had no idea what to think. We continued being wheeled to the "Angio-suite".

"No one who does good work will ever come to a bad end."
- Bhagavad Gita

CHAPTER 7: To angio-suite and back

It looked like any operation theatre which is fitted with a specially built X-ray machine capable of taking several pictures while the radiologist does the operation. At the door there was a nurse, and another person who called himself an X-ray tech. Then I met the anesthetist. He had explained before that he would give me just an intravenous injection, which does not put one to sleep but takes the pain away. It was possible to view the entire procedure, when the radiologist did it live. I was reassured.

Soon after Dr. Levitt, the radiologist, whom I had already met, explained the entire procedure in detail, including the risks and possibility of death. The chance though remote needed to be spelled out. It is curious, I had had to speak about side effects of the various medications we use, and several of them can cause death. I had had to spell this out to patients. It is always difficult to convince anyone that treatment can kill while one is living and has to volunteer to do something that might end their life. It is difficult to accept. It is difficult to explain that no matter how miniscule the chance that there is a chance nonetheless. Then I have to speak about life's vulnerability: just crossing the street, taking a bicycle ride, flying or even a peanut getting stuck in the throat and getting choked, hundreds of other totally unexpected reasons can cause death to help alleviate the anxiety.

When Dr. Levitt did utter death as a risk, I was perhaps not listening to him. I was repeating to myself what I have spoken to patients for years on the possibility of death from simple medical procedures or standard tested day-to-day medications. I was talking to myself for reassurance. The difference is I had no control over anything being done to me. I trusted the doctors, I trusted Dr. Levitt and most importantly, I trusted myself.

Dr. Levitt was a no nonsense person. As I was fully ready for his procedure, he started the procedure immediately. He introduced a cannula into a major artery in my right groin. I could see what he was doing. I did not have any pain, discomfort or any feeling at all. Dr. Levitt was giving a running commentary as he progressed. I could see the tube coming up to my heart, into the heart and into some small arteries of the heart. He took several pictures. I could hear the words 'Shoot, shoot'. I guess it was an assistant who was shooting as the doctor was selecting the appropriate condition to take pictures.

In the end, everything was over in about an hour or less. I was told to maintain pressure in my groin for the rest of the day and watch for any swelling at the site of the puncture in my right groin, where he introduced the cannula for the test. The Sister did put a heavy pressure bandage and cautioned me for bleeding or any swelling in the groin.

Dr. Levitt seemed happy with the test and said he would send the report to the cardiologist in the next hour or so.

I was very keen to know about the result since he did not volunteer any information and I resisted asking. Any way soon, I would hear from the cardiologist, regardless. Again, I was transferred on a stretcher and wheeled back to the cardiac ward and my room.

By 8:30 a.m., I was back on my bed. By this time, the staff had changed to a new team, but the sister-in-charge was there. After I settled down on my bed, Sister Thompson came and checked the pressure bandage for any evidence of bleeding or swelling. She was happy and asked if I was ready for breakfast. I was indeed, then came my hospital breakfast with my favorite black coffee. I was hungry and enjoyed the breakfast that was served.

By ten-thirty, my cardiologist came with his company. He apologized for the disturbances last night, due to the critical patient. He advised that I could be moved to a single room, but his preference was this particular room because it was close to the nursing station and having another patient in the room, the need for nursing staff to visit the room is more frequent.

I did agree. I was happy and critical patient's care did not bother me at all. The nurses and other support staff were excellent.

Then he brought up the report of my angiography, which was done earlier this morning. What he said, unfortunately, was that I had a few blockages. The radiologist did not think any of them could be expanded or kept open by placing a stent to keep the blockage open.

He had already spoken to the senior cardiac surgeon to see me and discuss the possibility of surgical bypass to improve the blood supply to my heart. He explained what is done in a surgical bypass, in stent placement and balloon dilatation. I was well informed about all these procedures but still I was happy to hear from him for my reeducation and assurance. We talked about the possibility of surgery, which he thought I should discuss with the surgeon.

He also reminded me that one more test remained, that is the MUGA scan, which is important especially for follow-up examinations.

He had a few more patients in the ward to see, juniors to instruct and students to teach. He said, "Expect to see the surgeon this afternoon or early evening; he will come after he finishes his surgery." He left with his entourage.

At around 5.30 p.m., the surgeon arrived. He was middle-aged, full of energy and enthusiasm with a very 'surgeon like' personality. He apologized for being late. He had had a couple of cases to finish. A heart surgeon's couple of cases means a matter of eight to ten hours if not longer.

"How are you feeling, sir?" asked the surgeon.

"Never better," said I. "Since I have been in your ward—I mean the cardiac ward—I have discovered what the real meaning of 'Feeling better' is. Before I was admitted, I did not feel sick except for a few days before coming here; you know the story. If I had the capacity to erase those few days from my mind, then I must admit, I feel so much better after being admitted than before. Although I never felt sick, I had no understanding what the real 'feeling better' feels like."

I thought that maybe I had confused the surgeon. It was indeed far from my reading. He quietly stared at me for a few long seconds, smiled and gently said, "Sir, medicine can do miracles. Unfortunately, we do not have the power to keep those miracles forever."

I realized what he was saying: that the effects of medications are temporary. I was heavily medicated at present, which had a short lifespan. "These are only stop-gap, but I need a more permanent solution, that is why I am here," said the surgeon, "to find a permanent solution, or as permanent as it can be done, or none at all."

Actually he did not utter these words; my runaway imagination threw a spanner on my never-ending optimism. Now I was eager to hear what he had to say, not what I would like to hear from him.

He started from the very beginning. He had examined my coronary angiography. He discussed with Dr. Levitt, blockage by blockage, and examined all the visible blood vessels of the heart and finally agreed with Dr. Levitt that none of the blockages were either expandable or stentable. So both of them, with my cardiologist, had come to a conclusion that a bypass, or what is known as "cabage" procedure, was my only option. However, the next morning, he would present my case to the rest of the group to obtain a decision.

"This is routine," he said. He promised to return the next day as soon as the meeting with the rest of the group members was finished. But he did emphasize that I must be prepared mentally to undergo the massive six to eight hours of surgery.

He left after a much too long day to go home to his family.

Early evening in the ward, the room was teeming with visitors who were well controlled and well disciplined. The ones I could see were in moods of extreme sadness to high exuberance. Everybody was trying to visit with their patient/relative/friend/colleague.

I was drowned in flowers, bouquets, 'Get well / get better/our prayers/God bless…' cards. Later, I had to ask the sister to take some of them to decorate some other parts of the ward.

Late in the evening, as I dozed off to sleep, some noises woke me up. A stretcher brought a young man to be admitted in the other bed. He was also awake but did not give the impression of a sick person. A robust man, obviously in distress, and several young friends or relatives accompanied him. He came in with several electronic gadgets attached to him and a couple of bags of fluid hanging from the infusion pole. He must have been sick. But he seemed too young to have a heart attack. He looked too healthy to be a patient of any sort. For half an hour or so hospital staff, doctors, nurses, and technicians from many units came and went after doing their bit. I could see a couple of monitors at work, which appeared to be routine. After a couple of hours, the crowd thinned to one young lady and hospital staff visiting sparsely. I was surprised to see the patient getting up and sitting on his bed whispering something to the lone lady. Quickly she got up and went out to return with the night nurse. All three chatted for a couple of minutes. I could not hear.

The Sister left and in five minutes a trolley lady wheeled a trolley full of fruits, sandwiches, various vegetable presentations, water, juices and a pot which might have coffee in it. The young patient and the lady had been looking at me with sadness and wondering what was wrong with me. Would I be able to go home or be stranded in here, where everyone was wondering what next?

Yet the young man was jovial, said good evening to me and asked how I was feeling, how my day was, what I had been admitted for, how long I had been here and many more questions.

I was interested to hear him, particularly his enthusiasm in spite of being in the cardiac ward, having been wheeled in from the ER. He must have had some form of cardiac-related emergency; that was why he was in the ER and now in cardiac ward. But what I see in him does not fit into the above scenario.

I replied to all his questions. But in the end I did say, "I am waiting to have a cardiac surgery, not sure when. But the medical treatments they are giving me in the hospital, the nursing care I am getting, other assistance and related support and enormous volume of 'Get well wishes', I am getting from all around, make me feel so well, as if I had never been so well before and make me feel like a fraud to occupy a bed. But my surgeon's words cannot lie. I am mentally preparing myself to undergo seven to eight hours of heart operation within the next few days."

"Thank you for sharing. You are lucky to be here; the surgeons are highly professional; the medical care is excellent—I can say next to none in the country. You will be all right after all is done, what they say they want to do.

"I was told you are a specialist, Doctor. Good for you. Not a bad idea for a doc to be sick from time to time, to appreciate the practice of medicine—what do you say, Doc?

"By the way, I am Freddy. I am well known to this ward — to the nurses, the doctors and other staff. I work as a bartender in downtown-rough area. I have been doing the job since I left college. They pay me very well and I love my job. I made many friends and very few enemies; to tell the truth, I can't think of anyone who would like to knife me, whereas in that part of the city drunk or sober 'knifing' other people any time of the day is a kind of pastime. After all, as you know, our city is known as the 'knifing capital' in the country.

"A few years ago, while working around midnight, I felt dizzy and passed out. I was brought to the ER at this hospital. After being examined by various specialists and tests finally they came to a conclusion that this is not a classical 'bartender's courtesy syndrome', that is, over-sampling of bartender's creations of various cocktails, Bloody Mary, Buck's fizz, daiquiri, high ball or hot toddy etc."

It is not unreasonable to assume a patient's condition is related to the job. In fact, he had a similar episode 3 years ago for the first time.

He was taken to the nearby hospital. They kept me for few hours and discharged me home with no specific diagnosis, but advised to see my own doctor.

Since then, he had a few similar episodes, some not bad, some worse. From the second episode he has been coming to this hospital and this is where they diagnosed him to have a rare condition as "Eisenmenger's Syndrome" and not the "Bartender's courtesy syndrome" that other specialists thought.

"Anytime I pass out, my friends bring me here as instructed. My cardiologist tells me I need surgery. I have seen the surgeon. I guess they are waiting for the right time to do the operation. I am well otherwise and carrying out my job perfectly and I am enjoying it just as much. Because you are a specialist, Doc, and we are sharing the same room, no one else better to whom I can relate my story."

Suddenly he pointed to the food trolley and said, "I was very hungry and had nothing to eat after my lunch of a few tuna sandwiches. The sister is kind enough to provide me with a trolley full of goodies. I invite you to share from this trolley, if you wish. Even two of us will not be able to finish a third of the supplies. You are welcome to join us."

I was impressed but politely declined since I had some tests to be done next morning, for which I had been ordered a light dinner, which I already had. He understood.

Now I could fit 2 and 2 together. The puzzle of being very sick with heart disease, yet without any distress and being exuberant, being a bartender made real sense.

By this time it was close to midnight. The Sister came to look us over and reminded us that it was indeed close to midnight and I was scheduled for a test at 7 a.m. We both went to sleep.

Next morning, a gentleman nurse, woke me up and reminded me that the orderlies would come to pick me up at 6:45 for the test. They would serve my breakfast after I returned.

I looked around; neither my bartending roommate nor his lady friend was there. The bed was neatly and tightly made up and tucked in. The side tables had a beautiful pot of flowers, as if welcoming my next roommate. Sister told me that "Freddy" and his lady friend had left. They did not want to wake me and apparently they were impressed by my "calmness", they said as they left and hoped to meet me again.

What a big difference between my previous roommate and the one who came last night. For the first one the room and his place were sadly empty, life full of despair, but last night a different story, a sick young man left with feelings of life, hope and a future.

I was getting ready for my next test.

CHAPTER 8: Surgeon' s final thoughts, meeting with my family

I returned to my bed by 9:30 a.m. after I had my MUGA test. As I was wheeled in, a technologist and a nurse accompanied me to a waiting area.

This was the section of nuclear medicine where tests and treatments were done with the use of radioactive chemicals in very minute quantities. Yet the procedures and techniques were highly organized, monitored and controlled to prevent the minutest risk of spillage at any point, from drawing into the syringe to injecting into the veins.

These had been a part of my professional activity. I was watching every step they were taking. At every level handling was meticulous.

In walked Dr. Davis, the Nuclear Medicine specialist. "Good morning, Dr. Nice to see you after a long time. Hope our tests will put you on the right track. You are aware of the procedure, yet I have to recite to you once for the process of protocol," said Dr. Davis.

She indeed went through the whole procedure once.

Then, as usual, I had to sign a consent form as a part of the procedure, stating that I understood what was involved, the risks and benefits, etc.

I got the IV radioactive stuff. Half an hour later, I was put on an exam table and a huge radioactivity monitor that looked like a solid pie was slowly brought down close to my chest. This counter gathered the concentration of radioactivity in my heart and transmitted to a computer to be transformed as images. I could have watched what the monitor was showing, but the counter was in my way.

Not a big loss.

After half an hour, the counting was over. Dr. Davis came in and said, "Looks good." She would send the images and reports to the cardiologist and also to the surgeon by the next hour or so.

The test was over. I was put back on the stretcher and wheeled back to my ward and my room.

My daughter and her husband came from the Cayman Islands, my brother-in-law and his wife from London and my brothers were waiting for their visas and were not sure if they could make it before the date of the surgery.

The Surgeon wanted to have a family meeting with the psychiatrist, psychologist, ICU doctor, social workers and other support units.

He came to see me at 11 a.m. and said, "The departmental team has advised to go ahead with the surgery as he (the surgeon) suggested." So he got the support from his colleagues and the institution. Apparently this is routine for all cardiac cases.

Then the serious talk began...

He said, "Sir, I do not need to explain but I must express all cardiac surgeries are risky. You will be under general anesthesia for up to eight hours. There will be an experienced team working during and for certain a length of time immediately after the surgery. Although we have huge experience every patient is unique and you are one of the extra unique ones, judging from our colleagues' concern and calls from other colleagues and friends abroad."

"This is just extra," he smiled. He continued, "But once we start, the entire team is focused on a successful and uncomplicated operation for every patient."

"If you're wondering, *What is my chance of recovery from the table?* I must say it is always 50/50. There is always a chance that we may not be able to wake you from anesthesia. There is always a chance that the surgery may become so complicated that we may not be able to get your heart pumping again." He chose to avoid the word "death" or could not use the word from his heart to a person he revered as a colleague and a teacher.

I reassured him like an old 'sage'. "I am sure you will do your best and the rest is in someone's hand. I have full trust in you and the team you have chosen to support you. I feel strongly that with your help my glass will remain always half full."

What my cardiac surgeon said about the outcome of their work, I could not help but recollecting once of the greatest Indian surgeons, with whom I had great privilege to be associated with as my primary mentor, Prof. Amiya Kumar Sen, outstanding surgeon, outstanding teacher, and outstanding leader. He was the Director of the National Cancer Center in Kolkata, Professor and Chairman of Surgery at the University of Calcutta and also RGKar Medical College, University of Calcutta. These credentials meant little to him, but in my opinion Prof Sen's affiliation to the credentials meant lots to the credentials themselves.

The reason I brought it up is because the day I left India for London from Bombay by Ocean Linear P&O Oceania (just over fifty years ago), Prof. Sen just happened to be in Bombay. I went to say goodbye to him. He was busy in a committee meeting and could not come out but sent me a message that he would meet me on the boat at 5 p.m. the same day. He had all details of my travel. I could not believe he would be able to come. I was waiting on the deck while the cabins were being prepared. The boat arrived from Sydney early morning and was expected to leave at midnight the same day.

Right at 5 p.m., I saw Prof. Sen climbing up the stairs close to the gangway. I was elated and ran toward him. As I approached, I touched his feet and expressed my deepest reverence, according to Indian custom. He was happy to see me. We found a spot away from the crowed side of the gangway and started to exchange our thoughts. I was the listener. I could clearly feel that he was reminiscing his old days and wanted to share some of his life's events with me. For the years I was associated with him, I had never had the opportunity to be so close to his heart.

The time came when the First Officer announced that all visitors should leave the boat in the next hour. There was a big crowd of people who started slowly to walk toward the jetty connector. As we were walking, we stopped and he said, "This is the real beginning of your life; no one knows where it will rise to. But I kept thinking that over the last 40 years of my life as a surgeon, I had treated hundreds maybe thousands of patients. Many got better and others did not. Many a time, I asked the question to myself, why people got better with minimal intervention and others did not; even with the best effort. I can't explain it. Is it lack of anything? But I think strongly, we must do the best we can, both professionally and with our heart and leave the result to happen, which is not in our control since someone else looks after the rest. So remember to do the best for your patients, for that matter anyone who asks for your help. Help with your heart, mind and hands and leave the result to happen."

For last fifty-plus years I have never forgotten Professor Sen's blissful words.

I saw a bit of Professor Sen in my cardiac surgeon. I felt blissful and pensive.

Then he met with my family members, whoever was there — my wife, my daughter, my son-in-law, my brother-in-law and his wife. He discussed everything with them and warned them to be prepared for the worst. They were shocked. After more or less one hour of family consultation, he left and asked my wife to get all the papers ready and clear, in the event of my death.

"We must make sure that there is no ambiguity, no uncertainty for transferring assets and rights."

Everyone was devastated, disturbed and stunned. Filled with emotion, they did not know how to proceed or what to do. My son-in-law called my accountant to start working.

My accountant is a close friend. Since I have landed in Canada, he has been with me for good or bad, sunny or thundery, day or night, always there to help and advise. He speaks the truth. It hurts, but I know he has no reason to hurt me, but has every reason to help me. He appeared within half an hour. That was at 9.30 in the evening.

We discussed and he tried to reassure me that this is standard in case of any risky surgery, to cause as little difficulty as possible in allocating the inheritance. It is safer this way. My accountant is the best person to advise the lawyers to prepare a declaration of inheritance or a power of will for the inheritance.

He immediately spoke to one of my lawyers and made arrangements to be at the hospital by 9:30 the next morning.

He left but all my family members were still there. My daughter's red eyes were getting redder. I could see she could barely hold her tears in. At last she said, "Daddy, you will be all right."

By that time it was 11:30 at night. I told them, "It is getting late; you all should go home and come back tomorrow when you all can come." They all left, lights were dimmed and someone switched off the main light on the ceiling.

I kept thinking, again and again, I do believe that my glass is always half full and never half empty. It has to be half full and can never be half empty. I tried to reassure myself. I said to myself, why do I need reassuring? There is no confusion. I will be a new human being after the surgery. Why shouldn't I be?

By this time, I had all necessary tests done to prepare for the surgery; only the surgeon now had to fix a date for the operation. I hoped to hear the date of surgery by tomorrow.

I went off to sleep. But the thought of uncertainty kept coming back again and again. What to do if the glass is half empty? It is just not the lawyer's business to act. But my life could never be half empty. I would never let it happen. Well, could I? Who controls this? How much power was that?

With these conflicting, bizarre and confusing thoughts, I guess I did go to sleep, preparing for nightmares to come, but I had none. I can't describe it without having any experience.

I was woken up at 6 a.m., for a wash up.

As I woke up, I saw a gentleman who had apparently been admitted into the other bed overnight. I had no recollection of him coming in and being admitted. Everything went without much noise or clicking of activities. On the other hand, I may have been too physically and mentally exhausted to be affected by the activities for his admission; coming and going of staff, specialists, nurses, technicians; none at all. Surprisingly there was no bottle of fluid hanging around him, no oxygen tubes or masks, no bleeping or blinking monitors surrounding him. He was sound asleep when I saw him next to my bed.

He was woken up by 7 a.m. for medication. So was I.

Doctor's rounds started. A resident doctor first came, asked me several questions, looked at my chart and listened to my heart, although the heart function is monitored live 24 hours a day. I thought it was rather out of practice. Modern medical training is to look at the chart, data, x-ray, scans, etc. Some even forget to look at the patients, ask names; even wishing good morning or good afternoon is missing. The young doctor said, "You are fit and well to undergo the surgery. The cardiologist will be coming in shortly to speak to you about their plan of surgery."

Soon enough the cardiologist entered, greeted me as usual, looked over all the records he had and listened to the young doctor carefully.

He then said everything seemed to be satisfactory. "The surgeon wanted to do the operation tomorrow, but the only available slot would have to be the second case of the day. He was not happy, so he moved you to the day after tomorrow as the first case, which starts at 7 a.m. That is better. The surgeon will come later to discuss further." The cardiologist also said he would meet separately with my family and discuss more personally (after all, he was a personal and family friend). They were all prepared and waiting.

After the ward round, my new roommate walked up to me, greeted me and asked how I was feeling. I asked him the same question. We were both in the same situation. I would be undergoing bypass surgery in two days' time. He had been admitted for pre-operative assessment and tests for valve replacement operation. Apparently, that was more complicated, took longer and also had a longer healing and convalescence time than bypass surgery. He had been waiting for more than two years to get it done. But due to various circumstances it was delayed and delayed. But this time hopefully, he says, it will be done and he will be able to join his "Half Marathon" race again. He was very calm and composed and stable mentally to undergo his major surgical operation. He looked well. I wished him well and a fast recovery to get back to his family. He said the same wishes for me.

In three days in the cardiac ward, I met three people as my roommate, with cardiac illness, different illness, different age and totally different attitude to their illness.

At around 11 a.m. the lawyers, two of them, and my accountant appeared together, more or less at the same time.

"The highest form of wisdom is kindness."
- The Talmud

CHAPTER 9: The lawyers and the final will

There were no further tests scheduled for me today, except to see through my finances, the final will and any other legal or financial affairs to regularize, in case of death or any other unpredictable situation.

There was a six-page document prepared by the lawyers with the help of my accountant.

The lawyers are expected to read the document to me and ensure that I understood every bit of the document that has been written. This is my last will and must remain confidential until I die. The custodian of the will has to be named, and I had no difficulty in sponsoring the senior lawyer to be the custodian. Most of the details of my assets and funds due to me and funds payable to others and other financial issues were given by my very capable accountant, who always has my best interest in mind.

We discussed the contents with the lawyers for more than an hour and named my wife as principal benefactor and my daughter as the joint benefactor.

The lawyers had to explain the rest of the contents again to me line by line, to remove any ambiguity.

I read the document again and again; many times by myself, to get a grasp of its contents. I did understand the contents. This was my will to protect my family, so that they do not have to go through any financial or legal harassment, should I die during or after the course of surgery or if I live a life of "Vegetable", unaware or totally out of control of myself. Very grim thoughts indeed. I have seen, certified death and consoled bereaved families on many occasions. These are very much part of my job. We do have to deal with death or dying patients and their bereaved families and friends. Never thought of my death or ever imagined that I would die some day or what would happen. All I could see was my daughter's red and teary eyes. I am not dead yet. Why was she crying; why was everybody so silent?

This was not real. After the lawyers did their bit, I signed on the dotted line, and made the lawyer as the custodian of my will, which he would break soon after my death in front of the entire family and anyone else who had a stake in my will. But I left strict instructions to the lawyer concerning whom he can ask to attend and whom he should not.

They left but decided not to give me a copy for the sake of security and confidentiality. I took their advice.

I saw all three of them leaving with their portfolio bags. One of them had my will and I had a horrifying urge to stop them, snatch the papers from them and tear it into pieces. With it they are taking away my existence, me as a person, a human being. All my life's work is shattered. I am empty, I am valueless and I am powerless. I did it as everybody advised me to do, my friends and many of my well-wishers.

Suddenly I lost all feeling, unable to think, blinded by my thoughts. A feeling of absolute uselessness and a feeling of slowly increasing detachment to everything worldly engulfed me. At that time, I thought the world had deceived me. Why should I not deceive the world by detaching from the world with a vengeance? I regarded my hard work, my solemn devotion to my profession, my family, my patients, my students and my friends. Where are they? Are they all telling me to give it all up? Is it cruelty or kindness?

They have gone away with my very existence, my very 'me'. Treachery or deception? Cowardice or heroic? I had no word for what has happened to me, my soul and spirit.

I could see them slowly walking away in the corridor, walking away from me. Suddenly they are gone. No sign of them. Am I yet dead? Or alive?

Of course I am alive. Very much alive.

As long as I am alive, those papers I have signed on scores of places are absolutely meaningless. After I die, if I do, I do not care what happens to those papers.

Of course I care; I care for my family, my sobbing daughter, my wife of thirty-two years, my brothers, sisters, friends and colleagues. I do care if my signature helps and protects them; that is all I have worked for my entire life. If I do die and leave this beautiful world, all those pennies I have hoarded, bricks put on one on top of other to build castles are not moving an inch to come with me. I came with nothing and leave the world with nothing, only bubbles of memories will keep bubbling and like any bubble will burst and disappear into oblivion. Maybe!

My anger, feelings of deception and sense of treachery all melted away. A feeling of absolute calmness prevailed.

I came down to the real world, away from the furious world of darkness and turmoil.

I guess I dozed off for a few seconds and woke up.

"Good morning, sir!" I heard from a very familiar voice.

It was my surgeon standing by my bed with my cardiologist and a whole host of young doctors. Doctors? Because their name labels on their white coats says so.

"You are doing well and ready for the surgery. I have to postpone the date from tomorrow to the day after tomorrow, so that I can put you first on the list and start early. I can determine when to start but I do not have full control when to finish. It generally takes anything between six and nine hours. I am expecting yours to be on the lower end."

"On my way in, I met your family," said the surgeon. "They are all eager to know the plan. I sat down with them for few minutes and explained the reason for the change of my plan for the day of surgery. They were all anxious but calm and waiting for the day and get it over with. You have been in this ward just over a week; generally it is two to three days. It is understandable why your family is anxious."

Then he walked to the next bed and talked to my roommate. They had various discussions about planning, his current state of his health.

I heard the surgeon saying that he has to delay his date by one day. It will be tomorrow, although his plan was for today.

The patient said, "Thanks very much. I have waited two years; I am sure another 24 hours will make no difference, if it suits you better. I feel well when I am in the ward, that tells about the care you and your team is giving me."

"Thanks for the good words, Mr. Benjamin. Our anesthetist will come again this afternoon to check you over for surgery tomorrow."

The group trotted out of the room to attend to the next patient in another room.

It was lunch time. My wife and daughter prepared my lunch at home and brought it with them. There was plenty for all five of us. I ate, chatted and got news from other family members. By 2 o'clock, they had to leave with a promise that they would return again in the evening with dinner.

"Had I not fallen I would not have arisen, had I not been subject to darkness I could not have seen the light.
- Midrash.

CHAPTER 10: What if I do not wake up?

The surgeon emphasized several times that the chance of success is 50/50; so the chance of waking up from the operation is also 50/50.

I kept reassuring myself that I have at least a fifty percent chance to have a successful surgery and get back to a normal life. At the same time I also have a fifty percent chance that I will fully wake up after the surgery. Not bad odds for such a risky act which potentially demands highly skillful hands and a fast thinking mind.

I trust my surgeon fully for his ability, his accuracy in judgment and superb dexterity.

But the question is will I wake up? There is a fifty percent chance that I will not wake up, as my surgeon said to me and to my family. That is the reality we must accept and live with.

What must we accept? That I will die? Yes, one must die, that is the only absolute truth, once one is born. We think of the death of others but very rarely of ourselves. So do I.

In my profession, death is one of the outcomes of our intervention in the process of life. I have written hundreds of death certificates for hundreds of people I have attempted to revive from death and failed, in hospital wards, in the ER, by the road side in accidents, in natural disasters and in war zones. I can't remember ever thinking what might happen to the person I have taken care of, who I gave all my physical, mental and possibly poorly perceived spiritual strength to help him start breathing again and failed. Never have my thoughts gone beyond confirming his death and writing the death certificate. What will happen to the person who I have known for months and years or gave all my strength to breathe again who has just died. I have never thought beyond the funeral, cremation or burial.

The person whom I just certified dead does not exist anymore and will never exist again. What happened to the person, beyond his body, if there is anything 'beyond his body' — that is where I stop to think. An absolute vacuum in my thoughts.

Let me look at the next patient.

As my cardiologist said, it might happen to me. I may die any time during or after the surgery. An absolute truth he uttered.

Yes, I might die. If not now, I will do so sooner or later. Death had never been in my thoughts, not for me. To me it is an absolute unknown; the fright of unknown comes with it. With the unknown comes the darkness, absolute darkness, the 'black hole' the never-ending expanse of empty space of the universe, even the perception of 'end' becomes blurred, as blurred as an illusion. There is nothing called the end, only the beginning. But what happened to people I declared dead, who I certified as dead? There is nothing beyond my certificate. They are just 'empty'. Or are they?

Yes, that will happen to me when I am dead. Of course I will not exist; I will be empty, an unconceivable emptiness, desolation, barrenness, a vacuum in the space and a sad feeling of dejection. Dejection from what, from whom if I do not exist?

It is not a strange feeling, that I never thought nor did it ever come to my mind again and again. What happened to people after I issued their death certificates? Now that I might be issued one, just emptiness, impenetrable absolute darkness, dark particles, black hole, blurred my thoughts and imagination.

I have walked the Canadian Tundra, trotted on Arabian empty quarters 'the rab al khali', deep equatorial forests in Africa, where sun never rises nor sets ever midnight, the desolation is supreme but as I started to ponder what is beyond my death certificate is absolute uncertainness.

In my job, when patients come with a problem, we need to go through a process of 'differential' diagnosis. We are expected to think of possibilities and gradually focus on the best diagnosis and proceed.

I have the absolute darkness, absolute unknown, absolute zero, absolute nothing after my death. This absolute nothingness is the reason why I am not yet clearly convinced what is beyond my death certificate.

That is scary, the confusion of perception and darkness of knowledge. I never thought what my patients might have been pondering, after I gave them the ultimate word, the only truth.

"I slept and dreamt that life was a joy: I awake and saw that life was service: I acted and behold service was a joy."

- Tagore

CHAPTER 11: The only truth

The one and only truth my surgeon gave is that I "might" die as a result of him trying to save me from my illness. Yes, I might die. What will my family think? I will not bother them with this inevitable question. I have worked out the financial security for them with my lawyer and accountant and I feel content to some extent. But how will they feel in a life without me? How will they feel to fill the eternal vacuum? I have no answer. How would I feel without them, if I am dead but still alive as some believe?

I am a scientist. At least my education, my training and my profession want me to believe so. As a scientist, I can only believe what can be proved by various tools available to scientists, to prove or reject the authenticity of any claim. Just as with the existence of life after death, continuum of living and many other beliefs, faith, teachings, doctrines, hypothesis, theories and astute scientific observational documents, nothing in the eyes of science is true until it is experimentally reproduced using accepted scientific methods.

One important shortcoming of this scientific dictum is the inadequacy of today's scientific measuring tools or criteria. As science progresses with its measuring tools and methods, the validity of scientific truth also changes. Until recently, science made us to believe that light is the fastest travelling phenomenon in the universe. Now science is telling us it is not so, because it could measure even faster travelling phenomenon, because it invented different instruments for measuring moving phenomenon in the universe. This inability of science's measuring or experimentally reproducing the claims has been a significant deterrent to human progress.

In the Middle Ages, science propagated the idea that world is flat and the entire universe revolves around the earth. Thousands of years before, Copernicus made science believe that the earth is in fact round and it rotates around its own axis. The sun is the center of our universe. Bhaskargupta the Indian mathematician-philosopher pronounced that indeed earth is round, its north and south poles are flat. He did it by observation and mathematical calculations. Science did not believe him and his astute observation. It set back Columbus's discovery of the new world by hundreds of years and Magellan's attempt to circumnavigate the earth was delayed by one thousand years. For thousands of years, the Chinese adopted acupuncture as a viable and effective means to treat various illnesses. Unfortunately, Western science rejected it as hocus-pocus, until very recently both extensive clinical trials and phenomenal advances in neurobiology have explained why "acupuncture" has an immense therapeutic potential. Science has a real problem of living with phenomenon that can't be proved or that can't be measured with its own measuring tools and measurement criteria.

If surgery or anesthesia stops my breathing, the doctors will declare me as 'dead'. That is where its measuring sticks or rules end. When I am writing another "death certificate", I will freeze, I will cease, because I have no idea what is after. I never needed to know.

As long as the patient is breathing, I know, I understand the patient, I know what to manipulate to keep him breathing, to keep him talking and make him walk. Once he stops breathing, he is beyond my influence. There is nothing I can do to make him breathe, speak or dance. He is lost to my sphere of influence. He is a phenomenon I do not understand, nor do I wish to go deeper to understand. I am helpless. Neither my training nor my education, years in medical schools and higher centers of learning have ever encouraged me to think about what happens after the CPR is abandoned. The patient is abandoned as well. For me the ignorance is absolute concerning what happens to the patient after he stops breathing and I have issued the death certificate. The ignorance is unfathomable; it is total darkness.

Is that what is going to happen to me? All the caregivers, doctors, nurses, family and friends will stop feeling my existence, an absolute vacuum, an unfathomable darkness. It is hopeless to try anything to turn around to stop me plunging into the 'nothingness".

I have no words either, beyond these thoughts.

So why am I here? What was my role, what did I do for my fellow people, why was I even born? Why is anyone born if we are destined to be in eternal 'oblivion' after a few years of life on this planet which we can see, touch, feel pain, sorrow, desperation and even cherish being here?

Again I have no answer.

Judaism has the obvious answer – 'This is it'. This is the only life we have, clean beginning and sharp ending. Nothing before, nothing after. We know nothing about 'before' and nothing after. That may be the reason hardworking, clever people accumulate their successes and become the most prolific and generous donors on earth. There is no other culture like the Jews who are extraordinary philanthropic benefactors. They do talk about immortality and resurrection with unclear tones and in ambiguity. That is fine, as long as this life on earth is fully realized to its maximum potential.

So I will be zero, after I stop breathing.

Hindus believe in rebirth and reincarnation of souls. Hindus believe that souls are an immortal and imperishable part of life. Hindus believe death is a natural process prior to rebirth, a breathing space to refreshing stop gap or temporary cessation of physiological processes, recharging the soul (the atman) for the next journey on earth. They believe each rebirth is a learning process and rediscovering the 'self', overcoming the paradoxical inconsistent behavior and thoughts. They believe after several rebirths, the soul is liberated from the body. Both the release of soul and its reincarnation into a new body do take a large piece of Hindu holy book "Srimad Bhagabat Gita". In Hinduism, the belief in reincarnation takes a major account of one's karma or activities in this life shaping the reincarnation or the next life.

We hear about people born with accurate memories of previous lives. Is that a proof of reincarnation? The evidence is numerous. But scientifically, this is neither measurable nor reproducible hence a scientific "non-fact".

I was born in the Hindu faith. My death is secured but 'after death' to me is uncertain; reincarnation hazy, confused. Planning impossible. Moksha is the ultimate destination of the soul, when my soul will ultimately be freed from the perpetual reincarnation. I am yet to conceive Moksha, yet to perceive Moksha. It is still a big unknown. That is uncomfortable, even scary. That is partly a perception about death, the "unimaginable unknown". I am led to believe that death is not the end, there is life after death, that life is more worldly, more keen than what I know, what I have seen, with my soul regained which detached from my body as I died.

So I get the reassurance there is life after death, but where is the proof?

Christianity believes in resurrection, that is, a new birth with a resurrected soul, as opposed reincarnation, which is the rebirth of the same soul. Christians believe in life after death, after which a day of punishment for all, then comes resurrection. A new person, a new body with the same resurrected soul.

I must believe in spite, of all my sins, after my death, I will be resurrected. Indeed, there is life after death. Jesus Christ was resurrected, so he helped many souls to be resurrected. Testaments are the testimonies. Western science is yet to prove resurrections and miracles. But I must live with it, interestingly for "Christ's" sake.

Other Christian faiths like orthodoxy, Seventh Day Adventists, Jehovah's Witness, Jesus Christ of Latter Day Saints, all agree that life after death is real, a part of the perpetuity of living.

Buddhists also believe in reincarnation, life after death. And after several cycles of reincarnations, back and forth, eventually we will achieve "Nirvana", complete freedom, detachment from the worldly body; the soul travels un-hindered to Nirvana. Nirvana, the concept, the place, the journey remains an illusion to me, however perfect it may be. The proof, the reproducibility and the science are missing. Maybe the actual tool for detecting and measuring is yet to be discovered.

Yet I can't reassure myself that there is life after death, that I may not be "Zero".

Islam also believes in life after death. Islam believes in continued existence of the soul and a transformed existence after the death of the physical body. After death, either we go to heaven or hell after judgment day. Specific and clear.

So I will not be a "Zero" after I die; there is life and may be in heaven or in hell. Science yet has a classical question to ask. Proof, reproducibility and measurements, —can define the scales of the parameters to measure.

The Zoroasters believe in after life.

The Sammans also believe in life after death. In fact, almost all spirit-based faiths accept life after death.

Yet science fails in each individual practice. Maybe it is asking the wrong questions and using the wrong tools to measure.

But some scientific studies originating in Northern China (Ref) and a recent one in the West, involving many nations both north and south of equator all uniformly confirmed the identical experience of people who have been resuscitated from death, involving thousands of individuals, numerous countries, races, cultures, linguistic and religious divides. In fact, across multiple socio-cultural, political and economic divide, the experience of all those who had near death experiences were identical.

The feeling of floating above one's body where one can see one's body from above. A dark tunnel, a bright light moving toward them, bright colors, crossing a river, travelling to different places, family, friends and religious figures surrounding to comfort them and to prepare for the journey. A sense of peace, tranquility, compassionate and sensitive, to others, the perception is more lucid and coherent than a real dream.

This is so uniformly universal, it is almost unreal. This is the near-death experience of all human beings who had it, and who could communicate. This is the strong evidence supporting the existence of life after death. Undeniably so.

So should I die, I can be reassured of the existence of life after death and a return to life after death. So I will not be 'nothing'. I will live along to continue a normal or a partially normal life.

On second thought, should these cross-cultural, cross-national, cross-social, across geography experiences be identical, then it may be unlikely to be a biological or a neuron-psychological reaction. As all human beings are on the same evolutionary scale, the near-death experience is possibly an evolutionary-pathophysiological reactive phenomenon rather than an individual physiological reaction to a near-death event.

Yet, thinking of all these again, in spite of huge socio-cultural beliefs that, there is life after death and death is not the end and may be the beginning of something new has made me more confused and more uncertain about the finality of my death.

So far I am yet to be convinced that my life will perpetuate even after my physical death. Do I want it? Not sure. Still the fear of uncertainty lingers, fear of darkness prevails, fear of unknown is daunting; some piercing rays of hope trickling through. I took several deep breaths and eventually stopped taxing my brain and fell asleep.

Before I actually fell asleep, I kept thinking deeply, how come all these years in my profession where I had to deal with death and dying, hundreds maybe thousands of death certificates after, I do not remember any of my patients having ever asked me or discussed with me about the real meaning of death and is there a life after death and if so how can I explain? The priests, the rabbis may be doing it in their terms but not necessarily what the patient wants to know.

After more or less fifty years in practice, this is indeed a revelation. They must be pondering, asking the same questions as those I am asking for myself. I have no answer for this for this question, neither for any of my patients nor for myself.

CHAPTER 12: The day of preparation

I woke up early feeling rested, less tense and less worried. I asked myself all the questions, I asked my doctors all the questions, and mostly I got a reply that made me content. The ones that had no answer, I convinced myself those questions are not for me. I can forget about them and plan the life ahead, whatever is left to handle. I still had those little transmitters attached to my chest, body and sides. They stayed well all these days and functioned well, as one of the sisters said. Morning rituals of washing up, making the bed and having the breakfast, medications after medications were all done on the dot. I felt well and energetic.

Then started a series of visitors from the hospital team. The supervising nurse, the social worker, the dieticians and the physiotherapist, one at a time like clockwork. In the interim the resident had come and checked me physically and completed his notes. He checked all my test results, ready for the imminent cardiologist's visit.

By 11 a.m., my wife, my daughter, son-in-law, brother-in-law and his wife all gathered, just to say good morning. They would be preparing the lunch and early dinner tonight. They had gotten permission from the nurse in charge and the dietician to entertain me before tomorrow's surgery. They were all talking and laughing with family news from various parts of the world: lots of "get well" wishes, some regrets for being unable to secure a visa to come from Nairobi or from Calcutta. One of my relatives thought it must be a joke; I couldn't be so sick for I would need such a major operation. Just a few days ago, I was trotting in Lima, Peru, driving in the middle of the ghastly night along the California coast from Los Angeles to San Diego. I said to all of them, that was a miracle. Until I collapsed on the treadmill right inside the Cardiology Clinic, I had no idea I was sick or that to fix it I would need my chest split wide open.

It was surprising to my friend cardiologist, my colleague cardiac surgeon, the radiologist and my friends all over. But to be in the 'great men's club', one must have a stent put in, single to triple or quadruple bypasses or at least a lowly pace maker. Maybe I will be with them soon or never ever arrive to their level if I do not wake up. I just can't shake it up, the very thought of not being able to wake up and disappearing unrecognizably into the oblivion of eternal darkness. The very thought of 'absolute blank' — what is going to happen to me after I die? This 'me' will be a non-entity. Even after so many metaphysical interpretations of the existence of soul and life after death, so many well-documented 'near-death experiences', nothing exists that is reproducible and measurable. During our life, most of the activities and events that take place are generally reproducible and measurable. The knowledge we get from all these pre-death phenomena are generally accumulated and utilized for betterment of the lives of all human beings and other living objects.

When Christopher Columbus set sail into the unknown ocean, he had no idea how his expedition would look. But he had a definite focus, which was to reach his destination, the East Indies, the land of knowledge and riches. But, as the wise people say, almost all scriptures teach that life does not end at death; the soul perpetuates. But to what end, if there is one? What is the destination? Where does the soul fit in the vast, ever-expanding universe? The expanding universe is real. But at least we know why is it expanding; will it ever stop? Will it arrive to reach its purpose of expansion?

Science is blurred. Metaphysics is reaching in to provide answers. Just answers but no proof. Without proof, answers do not exist. Souls do not exist. We do not exist after our death. That is what science says. So how on earth in writing death certificates I never asked what is after? Although, I know what is after when I prescribe antibiotics for chest infections and why I am doing so.

How was the only truth in any life, death, never put to the test to answer these questions, using the tools of science? I guess because we do not have any tools to do so, as yet; that is the truth.

I have to stop thinking. None of my answers, if I do get any, will be useful to my surgeon for tomorrow's operation.

By 6 p.m., after a very light dinner prepared by my wife and daughter, the room slowly became quiet. They had to leave; relatives and friends of my fellow patient in the next bed who is waiting for heart valve replacement the day after also left and some of them wished me well. Interestingly, in such a short period of acquaintance, we became friends and some of his relatives also took the cue from him.

After some preoperative medication, I went off to a deep sleep, only to be woken up by a male nurse. He quietly said, "Doc, it is 5:30 a.m. now; we have to get prepared for your surgery, which is scheduled to start at 7:30 this morning."

So what do I need to do?

"I will take you to the shower. I will shave all your body for the surgery, then I will help you to get a good total body scrub to rid of any bugs and any scabs with some antiseptic solutions and then help you to get dry. Then I will help you put on these sterilized disposable clothes. We have already changed your bed sheets. You will go back to bed until the stretcher comes to wheel you to the anesthesia room."

At this time, I felt like a sacrificial lamb being fully prepared to be offered to the gods for 'some good'. That is exactly what the priests do to make the animal fit and suitable to be offered to the deity, so that every ritual was met with utmost perfection.

I remember as a child growing up in a medium-size city in India, we had annual worship of the Goddess Durga which is a major religious event observed all over India, more so in the Eastern part. She is the all-powerful mother Goddess who visits the earth to rid the world of a ruthless, barbarous man, which she does and saves humanity from his oppression and torture. A part of her welcome is animal sacrifice, mostly goat sacrifice. Every year on the eighth day of Durga's arrival, a goat is sacrificed. Before sacrifice, priests clean the animal, rub essences and chant holy hymns while incense is burnt. After the animal has been inducted for the ritual, small ones are carried by the priests while big ones are led to the sacrificial mound.

Hymns are chanted, bells are rung, holy drums are played, incense is burned, and fire burns in the pyre as part of the ritual. Just before the sacrifice, a curtain is drawn to keep the sacrifice process out of the public eye. As it is being done, more hymns, more prayers, more bells and drums are played to bring the sacrificial process to a euphoric height.

Now, I wished I had the sensitivity to look at the face of the animal, their feeling, and what they thought about what was happening? If I looked at the mirror now, I could find some clue.

In some cultures, humans were sacrificed, beheaded in the name of piety and in the name of a god. I can feel what might be going through their mind. By now, I feel absolutely like a sacrificial animal or a person whose beheading is imminent.

I put on the sterile disposable garments. The nurse slowly walked me back to my bed and said, "Doc, you may rest for a few minutes; the stretcher will be coming shortly."

I could barely hear him. A sense of absolute peace, nothingness, even a feeling of weightlessness, complete detachment from everything worldly and a sense of beauty came upon me. I am ready for anything. Nothing can harm me, as if I did not exist. I even forgot where I am. Why am I here? What am I doing here? In fact, I did not care.

I guess I dozed off for a little while, when the ward sister woke me up. "Doc," she said, "the time is right; the stretcher from the OR is here. You need not get up; they will roll you out from the bed to the stretcher, and you will even not know that you have been moved out of your bed onto the stretcher."

When I was rolled out of the room, the sister accompanied me to the anesthesia room and reassured me that everything would go perfect, like clockwork. "You are being operated on by one of the best cardiac surgeons in the country." She wished me well.

When she was about to leave, I said, "Well sister, I will see you after the surgery then." I thanked her for all she and the rest in the ward had done.

"Immediately after the surgery, you will go to the ICU ward," which I was already told. "When you are released from ICU, I will certainly come and visit you in the Cardiac Surgical ward," she said and left.

I was in the anesthesia area. The anesthetist came and greeted me and quickly went through the procedure he was going to carry out. I was given some medication in the ward and I was feeling sleepy. A nurse hung some bottles and attached some monitors. The anesthetist said, "Just a small prick; you will not feel anything after that."

Indeed, I had absolutely no recollection after the light prick.

When I woke up, I was in the ICU. I do not remember seeing so many monitors, so many gadgets attached to any hospital bed. I looked around. I recognized my wife and daughter leaning over me. There were anxious smiles on their faces. They were happy to see me awake and speaking. I asked them the time. It was 5 p.m. My wife said, "You came out of the operating room just at 4:30 p.m."

All I could remember was that I was at the anesthesia room at seven in the morning. I have absolutely no recollection of those intervening 10 hours.

An X-ray technologist came with a portable X-ray unit. They said it was routine to do a chest x-ray after my type of surgery. *I have no problem,* I thought. My wife and daughter had to go out. They have been waiting since 7 a.m. with my son-in-law and brother-in-law. They all look seriously exhausted. I told them to go home and rest.

The radiographer took several x-rays from different angles and said that he would return in two hours to do a follow up. "This is routine," he said.

I went off to sleep. I had no discomfort, no pain and no uneasiness; I felt really rested and comfortable with a heavenly peace and solace. I was surrounded by love, happiness and blessings. No enemy, no anger, no hatred, no feeling of vengeance, no frustration. I know I am still alive and breathing and lying on an ICU bed.

What happened to all the doom and gloom, the hell and darkness? They are gone. I do not want to bring them back. This real 'me' is happy and I want to live forever.

Suddenly, I thought, is this the life after death? How can it be? I am still alive. Is there a "life after death", even when we are still living in this world?

Chapter 13: Re-operation

Apparently at 11 p.m., I had a third chest x-ray. I was completely unaware of the second x-ray. The findings of the second one did not look good. The shadow that was found in my first chest x-ray a couple of hours after I came out of surgery had apparently increased in size. So a third one was done. The finding of the third X-ray was even worse. It was larger, meaning that whatever was causing the shadow was active and progressing.

I could barely hear someone say that the surgeon would be here soon. I was always happy to see my surgeon anyway. I kept going in and out of consciousness. I was hearing things that were not spoken and not hearing things that I was meant to hear. Yet it was a feeling of deep peace.

I do not know how much later, I could clearly hear, "Sir! Sir! How are you feeling?" I saw the face of my guardian angel stooping over me and many other angelic faces standing around my bed. Again I heard, "Sir! Sir," then, I think I really woke up. I saw my surgeon, the anesthetist, one of the ICU consultants and my friend, a retired heart surgeon, all surrounding my bed. All the angels were replaced by people I knew well. This was real. I was surprised and somehow perplexed to see all of them around me. Then again, "Sir! Sir!" my cardiac surgeon was trying to speak to me.

I said, "It must be close to midnight; you are supposed to go on holiday tomorrow. What are you doing here?" I was fully awake and aware of my surroundings: I was in ICU after having a heart operation. The surgeon and the rest of them were looking grim.

The surgeon said, "We have been monitoring your progress with chest x-ray, which you have already seen. I am afraid there is leakage and bleeding at the operation site, which is not rare and can be fixed. That means I have to take you back to the theatre again and seal the bleeding spot. It will be a matter of a few hours again. Unfortunately, there is no alternative and we must go in as soon as possible."

"I would like to start no later than 1 a.m.; it is now 11:45 p.m. I have informed the anesthetist and rest of the team. We will take you to the theater by 12.45 am. I will make your family aware of this unfortunate development; I expect some of them to be here."

I had no reaction. Now the "Doctor me" took over. If there is any internal bleeding, let them go in and stop it as soon as possible. The surgical wounds are still very raw and young; he can reopen through those incisions to access the site of bleeding. I was totally unaware of what went on during my first operation, which went for nearly nine hours. Another few hours on the table under anesthetic will make no difference, as far as I am concerned. I have no fear, no concern, and no distress for the re-operation. I felt sorry for the surgeon and his team. My wife and the rest of my family all left around 9 p.m. with a sigh of relief that I woke up and was able to speak normally. I had no sign of any stress or distress, but when they heard about the second operation, they would be totally devastated.

Indeed, they were. They told me afterwards, after nine hours under anesthesia and then again for how many hours for the second one, they were all stunned and stoned, believing that is it. When they met the surgeon just before the second operation, he looked completely exhausted, haggard but with high spirits, and explained the reason for the second operation. It is not rare that he had to open up patients twice on the same day. Most of them did well. It would be much worse to "wait and watch", with a big blood clot pressing on the surgically injured heart and lungs and pressing on the breathing pipe called the trachea. He would fix it immediately rather than hoping it would take care of itself. The second operation took another three hours to finish. By the end he looked tired as hell but spoke like a wounded soldier who just won a battle. That is what my brother-in-law, who was waiting in the lobby to get the news from the surgeon, told me. They were cautiously relieved and returned home at 5 a.m., as did the surgeon.

By the time I arrived back in my ICU bed, it was 5 a.m. They took one chest x-ray at 6 a.m. and another at 8 a.m. The surgeon returned to check the x-rays and was satisfied that there was no more bleeding. He reassured me and wished me a fast recovery. He gave all responsibilities to one of his senior colleagues who would be looking after me while he went on his planned holidays for two weeks to Tenerife, although a day later. At least his family was happy.

Something strange happened after I had the first chest X-ray. I thought I went off to deep sleep. A few minutes later I woke up and found myself floating near the roof, looking at myself lying on the bed, still breathing. From above I could see everyone in the ward, the nurses and other workers, running around minding their own business. Some doctors examining, nurses medicating, all known faces, all known and real activities. I even could clearly see a young doctor getting information about me standing by my bed and speaking to me. In reality, I witnessed that while I was floating near the ceiling. I floated here and there, but never out of the sight of my body on the bed. I felt again so peaceful, so content, happy, detached, cleaned of all animosity, vengeance and hatred, as if I was in a beautiful, different world. But I was not; I was in the same room with the same people who were looking after me. I could see my body was on the same bed and seemed to be speaking to the nurse and the doctor, the anesthetist—this was all happening in real time, while I was floating above and watching myself and other activities. I floated around the ward, suddenly came close to myself. I was not sleeping; I was breathing normally but my face was full of serenity and looked angelic, as if I was in eternal sleep while I was still alive in the human world.

Suddenly this floating me disappeared, as the x-ray technician started to take another chest x-ray at eight o' clock in the evening for the surgeon to make further decisions. I was perfectly comfortable on the bed, when the surgeon gave me the good news that the bleeding had stopped.

I told him to have a wonderful holiday. He departed with his best wishes and "prayers". I slept all day the next day. My folks said afterwards that it is not surprising that I slept all day since the smell of anesthetic agents coming out of my breath was so strong that they felt giddy and confused as they sat close to me for 5-10 minutes. There is no way out of it. Almost thirteen hours under heavy anesthesia and twice splitting of my chest open. It was better that I was breathing something I breathed out that gave giddiness and a state of confusion, than if nothing; even I did not breathe plain, pure air.

In the evening the cardiac surgeon, the ICU doctor and the cardiologist told me I had recovered well enough to be moved to the surgical post-operative ward, a different ward than where I was admitted. I was feeling well indeed, thinking I might even go home, if they wanted. They normally keep the patients in the ward for three days, while teaching physiotherapy, advice on dietetics, change in lifestyle, mental and psychological engagement and proper use of complex therapeutics of cardiac medications.

With this information and advance warning of "the nature of things to come", I was moved to the post-operative cardiac surgical ward.

"Tragedy should be utilized as a source of strength."
- Dalai Lama.

CHAPTER 14: Post-operative recovery

Patients who have cardiac surgery are sent to the post-operative ward within one to two days of surgery. The whole idea is to raise the nursing level higher with a planned education program for rehabilitation.

I arrived in the post-operative ward, delighted to see my roommate from the cardiac medical and pre-assessment ward who had a valve replacement surgery the day after I had mine. He was fast asleep or under the influence of medications and hours and hours of anesthesia. He did not look distressed or in any discomfort.

I was put to bed and tucked in. Soon after medications, pills and IV drips continued. I had more bells and whistles attached to my chest. These were transmitters of my vital signs, like blood pressure, breathing rate, pulse, continuous monitoring of my ECG and blood gasses displayed in a screen, outside within close vision of the nursing station. I could even see the activities being displayed in the screen. I could see my ECG pictures were erratic, but I did not feel any different. It is an interesting movie, although even being in the business I had difficulty in comprehending all the theatrical show going on the screen, using my data and vitals.

Around 10 a.m., not the surgeon but the rest of the team appeared. They were well informed with most of my progress except what was going on in my lungs. I was glad to see the most senior in the group grabbed his stethoscope, percussed my chest and listened to my lungs and breathing front and back, and behaved like a real doctor, not one who treats you with CT and MRI, figures and pictures on the monitor, without even looking at you or even asking how you are feeling. This kind of behavior is noted by many patients, who express their agony and concern, but in this corporate world, even doctors are tied with dollars and dollars tied with time. What you can do or can't do during your clinical hours is controlled by men who only can count with their nose all the time on the pages of their ledger books.

I give my most venerated salutation to the group of doctors in Ontario, Canada, who revolted against inhuman, unethical, barbaric and oppressive ruling of medical practice thrust on doctors by the so called CEOs, who even can't spell 'sickness' or 'insanity'.

The general concern and empathetic attitude of the team pleased me beyond my expectations. After the team's full enquiry, they left, suggesting a chest x-ray to be done the same afternoon. The marching of medication continued. Most of the medications were delivered through the intravenous drip, which I came attached to from the intensive care unit. But some must be given orally. I did not ask about all the medications I was getting. Most important is that even after two major surgeries which went on for nearly thirteen hours, I had no discomfort, until I moved, coughed or took a real deep breath; then I could feel the sutures and some escape route of tubes draining my chest which came out through my upper abdomen or the stomach area. I did not realize these tubes were to relieve pressure from my chest and heart. I thought these tubes were feeding tubes going into my stomach. Instead of putting inside they were draining from inside. The bells and strings were still attached to my chest and to my surprise, some of them were also attached to my ankle. These were all transmitters, measuring or monitoring, some of my physiology, displayed on a screen just outside my door, which was in my full vision. There were six splits in the screen displaying live telling whether I was alive or at risk of being dead or dead. Some of them showed peaks and troughs in graphs, others changing numbers, some changing colors but none making any kind of noise or sound. It was just like watching a TV screen at play.

Sometimes I got engrossed watching the drama on the screen. Sometimes it was not so interesting, so I looked around for my 'interesting' fix. It was so different being an 'inmate' in an acute surgical ward than being a visiting staff or consultant or even being a resident doctor. One cannot fully feel or understand the pulse of the ward, the bed, the environment, the excitement and the drama that goes around in the ward throughout the day which does impact on patient's progress, forward or backward, upward or downward. Being in the ward on a bed did make me understand the difference in impact on me as a visiting doctor or for that matter any visiting staff or a resident doctor and being a patient.

As a doctor, I never thought of the ward as an "agent" or a 'therapeutic tool' actually helping or hindering, synergizing or antagonizing my efforts of healing my patient. The influence of the ward which not only constitutes the materials and the ergonomics, but also the attitude of the medical staff makes the ward a healing tool that is frequently missed. We put too much stress on the procedures, the medical potions, nursing care in the ward as the only help patients get on their way to health but fail to grasp the ergonomics and complex attitude that plays a significant role toward the patient's recovery. Having been a patient in a hospital, the effect of a clean, tidy well-maintained ward, along with happy, positive, energetic and encouraging staff, did make my days better than if any of the two components or both are lacking.

In our professional training, a sense of boxed-in discipline may be inappropriate at times; we fail to appreciate the reality but fall for the routine. Our horizon of appreciating what impacts on a patient's healing in a hospital setting, other than medication, direct nursing care and orderly lifestyle, needs to be broadened should we envisage optimal benefit of hospital admission. I never thought a bouquet of flowers near a patient's bed or the smell of a pleasant aroma or a painting of the rising sun in the Sahara or the South Pacific and gentle Baroque music in the air and smiling, encouraging staff, might have a profound impact on patient's journey to healing, while admitted to a hospital bed.

Now I do.

The rest of the day went by with visits of various trainers as mentioned before.

At around 4 p.m., my daughter and son-in-law came with tears in my daughter's eyes. I asked her, "Why are you upset?"

"I am upset," she said, "to imagine leaving you so soon after such a horrendous and marathon surgery. But we must return to our routine, back to work. Our flight lives at five the next morning. But if you see tears, some of them are tears of joy. At one point, we all had the 'unspoken' fear that we might lose you for the second surgery. But somebody relieved us of our fear and distress and gave us tears of joy. I feel confident you will get better and as soon as the doctors let you fly, you will come and spend some of your convalescence with us in Cayman."

We bid farewell; as she continued to wipe her eyes and left.

By 5:30 p.m. dinner arrived. They did send me a choice of menu before and I had to tick whatever I fancied. I had to forego my wife's homemade diet for tonight. The dietician was uncertain if I could be allowed outside food tonight. Apparently my non-cooperating lazy bowel and bladder were the medical staff's concern.

I ate what I could, not knowing what I was eating and what I ate. I can describe the food as "Algebraical", all signs and signals, not being able to visualize what it really represents. Anyway, I had my pre-bedtime medications and was tucked in by a nurse, hoping to fall asleep since being heavily medicated. I must have fallen asleep.

At one point, what time of night it was or early morning of the following day, I thought I was dreaming. In my young days, I had travelled in a 'sleeper' overnight train several times. In those days, train was the best way of travelling. In the daytime, you sit by the window and watch the landscape and the world pass by you. At night, one caretaker comes in and makes your bed to rest, while the train is slicing through the darkness toward wherever it is supposed to go. The train makes mini-jolts at every winding of wheels. Whether one is sitting or sleeping on a comfortable bed you will hear the sounds and feel the jolts, the continual rhythmic musical sound, until the train comes to a halt. These rhythmic musical clacking sounds produced by the wheels and the rails not only put you to sleep but also rock you on the bed throughout the night, making you feel like a baby in its mommy's arms. This is a memory I had of this sensation traveling in Indian and British trains.

In the evening after I went to sleep, I felt that I was travelling in a night train somewhere in the world, rolling and rocking gently as the train rushes forward. I thought, *If the feeling is not real, let me enjoy the dream of my past travel in night trains.* Sometimes the tossing and rolling were intense but still felt like a dream.

At one point I woke up and realized my body was shaking rhythmically; I was panting. Soon I realized it was not a rolling night train, but my fast and hard running heart that was shaking my whole body with each stroke of my heart. When I woke up to reality, I saw four heads leaning toward me. One of them was the Resident, the sister on duty, my friend the consultant cardiologist and the other face I vaguely recognized and the anesthetist who put me to sleep for my heart operation.

They seem to be relieved, seeing me wide awake. The cardiologist said, "We have been monitoring you for the last three hours. Your heart has been running too fast, which can happen after a heart operation. But if it went on for too long it is not good for recovery from the surgery and can be dangerous to life. That is why I requested our anesthetist friend to come and help us to calm your heart down. It is now almost back to normal. So we must make sure this does not happen again."

"Oh! That is what happened, thank you for saving my life," said I. But I had to tell them I was fully aware of what was happening for last two-three hours. But to complete the feeling, I did tell them about my subconscious awareness—I felt I was on a night sleeper train travelling from Calcutta to

Puri, one of the holiest places on the east coast of India, which I had done several times, as student.

"The fact," said my cardiologist friend, "That you have had no bowel action nor urine flow for nearly last four days does not help in these situations. We are arranging to give an enema and put in a urinary catheter as soon as the day breaks."

"That is fine," I said. I thought, *I have ordered enemas to hundreds of patients and passed catheters even more. So what is the difference?*

Anyway, what a surprising compromise. My wayward running heart, which was about to fail of exhaustion with a pleasant memorable travel to one of the holiest places, can't get the connection. Could this have been my last journey out of this world, put on hold by my caretakers at the hospital?

A strange feeling, I never stopped to ponder.

"There is no darkness but ignorance."
- William Shakespeare.

CHAPTER 15: Days in the ward

I indeed fell asleep—no rocking, no dreaming just a clean, deep, uninterrupted sleep. I woke up with a voice calling, "Sir! It is 7 a.m., time to wake up. I need to give you a towel wash. You are going to have an enema and in place a urinary catheter, since neither of these has worked for the last four days. After the wash, I will give you the enema," said the male gentleman nurse with a voice of confidence but polite enough to earn my respect. He went on to say, "If the result of the enema is satisfactory and if we manage to give you a good clean up, then another nurse will come to place the catheter to release retention of urine, which is not uncommon after any major surgery and prolonged anesthesia."

 I nodded to agree with him.

He prepared me to put the contents of the enema bag into my bowel. I was all ready for the inconvenience.

Suddenly it occurred to me, this was the first enema I have ever received. My understanding is to examine one's bowels (rectal examination) first, before giving an enema. The reason for constipation may be due to many reasons other than sluggish or lazy bowel, which is most likely the cause of my constipation. But I do not remember anyone performing a rectal examination on me. *Never mind*, I said to myself, *let the doctor and his staff do what is best for me.* Someone may have done, while I was heavily sedated or while I was in deep sleep. I must say it was not painful, but uncomfortable and deeply embarrassing. Emotions aside, I went along with his instruction. He started slowly, almost quarter of a liter of fluid deep into my bowels. I relaxed and took a deep breath from time to time, as much as I could. We waited for half an hour and to his disappointment, the first attempt was not successful. He let me know that he would try again with a different solution. I was all for it. Constipation is not pleasant when it goes hand in hand with a bladder that can't get rid of urine.

He repeated the procedure, inserted the nozzle higher and put another quarter of a liter of fluid into my bowel. Amazingly, within five minutes my bowels started working and within the next ten minutes, I had evacuated my bowels to his satisfaction and to mine as well.

Now I could feel the tense full bladder. I tried to empty my bladder myself, but using all tricks the nurses had in their books, nothing worked.

About half an hour later, a young nurse approached me said she would be the one who would catheterize me to empty my bladder, which was well distended and getting to be tender. She prepared me for the procedure. She was smart, full of confidence, and explained the procedure to me. I felt hopeful that relief was forthcoming.

The beginning went well. The catheter slid easily up to a certain distance, then she had difficulty in pushing it farther. She tried to manipulate the catheter in various directions. After a few tricks the catheter was progressing slowly but was getting painful and uncomfortable. She continued to push the catheter slowly. I could not feel that the catheter had gone any further into my urinary passage. The more effort she made to introduce the catheter into my bladder, the more painful the process was becoming.

By looking at the length of the catheter outside the urinary passage, I thought it should be well inside my bladder, but there was no sign of urine released from my bladder. By this time the pain was becoming uncomfortable. I suggested squirting some saline into the catheter to confirm its patency. By this time she was getting unhappy. She indeed squirted some water into the catheter, and the water was flowing reasonably freely. Suddenly we noticed it started to come outside the urinary meatus (opening).

It was clear to me that the catheter end, instead of moving forward into the urinary bladder, curled backwards and was coming outside. This can happen even in the most experienced hand. The most important thing is to realize the situation without struggling to push it harder.

She did and gradually pulled out the catheter. The discomfort lingered. I was happy to give it a retry. With a different type of catheter with some lubricant and firm but gentle maneuver, the mission was a success. Almost two liters of urine was drained for my relief and comfort. The catheter was kept inside and attached to a bag, for urine to flow freely into the bag.

It was an experience I will have difficulty forgetting not entirely because of my personal experience; generally male patients' urinary catheterization used to be done by male nurses or young male house officers. I was happy to see the barrier has been lifted.

I returned to my bed with drips, catheter, several bells hanging from my body and two tubes attached to a collecting bag coming out of my upper abdomen just above the belly button. The quantity drained in this bag was measured daily. I understand these two tubes are draining fluid from two sides of my chest. By the third day in the ward, the collection in these bags was almost negligible and the tubes were removed the next day.

The next evening the resident, after his evening round, having discussed with the consultants, ordered the catheter removed. I was able to pass urine freely but still had some stinging sensation.

The rest of the day went by through various discussions and education plan.

After the bowel and urinary issues had been tackled, it was now time to work out a discharge plan. I needed advice on various aspects of my lifestyle after I was discharged and returned home.

By 10 a.m., the team from the Cardiac Surgeon and cardiology came. One of them, the senior clinical support, seemed to be enquiring about my condition. He mentioned about last night's episode of my runaway heartbeats, which had been effectively controlled by the team.

"Current data in the monitors are all fine and stable. The lab results are as expected," he said. He apologized for some difficulty with the enema and catheterization, but expressed relief as the procedures were successfully executed with desired results. He seemed to be well informed about my condition.

He checked the amount of urine in the collection bag and said, "It looks good; we will remove your urinary catheter today. Hopefully you will be able to pass urine normally." Then he checked the bag draining fluid from my chest through two tubes, just above my belly button; there were a few cc of clear straw-colored fluid in it. No bleeding or clots or sediments in it.

Then he listened to my chest, felt my abdomen and said, "All seems to be well; we may be able to remove the chest tubes tomorrow morning, if not tonight. There is no rush." He asked about hospital diet and sleep and if the bed was comfortable enough. I was generally happy with all the special attention I was getting. All the staff were very kind to my family, responded to all their queries and generally tried to reassure them; they went out of their way at every step.

After the visit by the medical team, came the dietician with the menu for lunch. This didn't happen in the other ward, where I was admitted before my surgery. There it was a straightforward menu — what was to be served for the day. But today the menu had choices. The dietician asked about my preferences and any of the items that I did not like. The list was well balanced and well "caloried", almost academic.

I had to tell her I am possibly intolerant to wheat, white or brown; they all give me muscle and joint pain. I also said, "I do not tolerate milk and milk products."

"Really!" she said and asked if I mentioned it to previous dieticians. She admitted, "The unit is careful about serving milk and milk products. Any information they record at the time of admission about allergies and any dietary intolerance. What I am saying is against the popular belief of brown and multigrain breads are superior to white or processed wheat products."

"Certainly not for me," I said. "I do avoid them if I can, at any cost."

"So you have been eating brown bread; that is what we cater to all patients. We will substitute wheat with rice for you from today."

I said, "Most of the time food came from home, except when I was in ICU and the last two days in this ward. For fear of infection and imbalanced makeup of food brought from home or outside, they restrict such practice. However, this can be changed for a good reason."

The dietician seemed reasonable and considerate. She asked me, "How many people out there are intolerant to wheat? I had no data on it but remember reading in some popular magazine that forty percent of world's population is intolerant to wheat and wheat products, which may be the cause of so many chronic illnesses."

That is a huge number of people who may be harmed by wrong diet. She was concerned and promised to look into the available literature and if she found any supporting evidence, she would discuss this amongst her colleagues, for possible revision of policy.

"That will be very helpful," I said. "There is some amount of gluten and MSG in wheat. By consuming it day in and day out, the cumulative effect may be considerable. I know rice has minute quantity of gluten and MSG, but the amount is too small to cause much cumulative effect over many years."

A clear understanding of tolerance of our two mostly widely adopted staple foods and their appropriate use may be a way to control many chronic diseases, improve health and productivity, and save money to take care of serious illnesses.

I was pleased I had the opportunity to vent one of my dietary anxieties to a professional, who was willing to listen and took my point seriously and followed it through.

From that day on, I had rice as my staple for rest of my days in the hospital. I do understand in an institutional setting, it may be a huge task to individualize dietary requirements. But if it can be planned and implemented the gain may be huge, not just during hospital admission but a source of life-changing education.

After the dietician left, another young lady came, a physiotherapist, specialist in rehabilitating patients after major heart and lung operations.

"Good morning, sir!" she said. "I am Tina. I will be your physiotherapist until you are recovered."

"Good morning Tina," I said, "happy to see you. I am sure I can do with lots of your help. Thank you for coming."

"Normally," Tina said, "we make our patients mobile from the second day they come to this ward, but in your case we will delay by a day because of your cardiac event last night. That is the advice from the cardiologist. That means your discharge will be delayed by a day or two. Tomorrow I will walk with you in the corridor for a couple of times, then you will do it on your own four or five minutes at a time, three to five times a day. First I will walk with you, and then I will help you to use the walker. When you feel confident, then you may walk without any help. Most important is to make sure you do not get any chest pain or overwork yourself to become short of breath. If any of this happens, you immediately tell the nurse or nurse's aide or anyone close to you to inform the nursing station. I don't expect it to happen, but I must tell you so. Tomorrow, I will give you a basic exercise plan, which you will continue to do at home." She gave me a booklet of instructions and diagrams for exercises I was expected to do at home after I was discharged. "Perhaps you would like to go through it and let me know if you are unclear on any of these."

"I have no problem with that. Thanks again and I will see you tomorrow," I said.

"Around 11 a.m.," she said and departed.

In the meantime, several nurses visited, sometimes with little paper cups with tablets, sometimes with thermometer, since the automated recorder did not monitor my temperature, sometimes checking my pulse and blood pressure, not trusting the automated recording devices.

By 2 p.m., I took the courage to walk to the wash room to pass urine. They had removed the catheter earlier. It was difficult to start, but when it started it was uncomfortable and painful. I thought it must be due to the trauma from catheterization. I did not produce much urine, but the feeling to pass urine lingered. I returned to my bed and was helped by a nurse in to it. My chest scar was still raw, as were the abdominal scars. I had several transmitters attached to my chest, transmitting all kinds of information displayed in the monitor just outside my door. I had little pain or discomfort in moving. I felt content and expected a fast recovery from such a major event in my life.

"This is a brief life, but in its brevity it offers some splendid moments some meaningful adventure."
                                                                    - Rudyard Kipling.

CHAPTER 16: Days in the ward (2)

Hustle and bustle in the ward continued. Around 3 p.m., an elderly lady came and introduced herself as a social worker, Susan, working in this hospital for more than twenty years. She was aware of my association with this hospital.

"Glad to hear and I feel relieved that you will be looking at my social affairs."

She burst into laughter. "Oh no! I would like to make sure you have enough support and if we can help you in any way," she said. She had already spoken to my wife, my daughter and my relatives visiting from abroad. She did discuss briefly with the cardiologist, who is a friend of mine, from a social point of view. She realized that we had a host of community support, but she was wondering if when all my close relatives left, my social contacts would remain as supportive as they all are now. Yet she promised that she would visit my house and see how her team and the department can help. She did mention that I would not be able to drive until I got a green light from my doctors. Until then we must secure a driver or a ride if none of my family or friends are available.

"This is not really a problem. Our team can even help you with shopping and some essential medical chores, for example, arranging hospital visits, prescription refills, pick up and deliver to your door." She did say over the years, she has come across many communities and generally felt very happy to see the strong community bond, community feeling, community support and your community offers. "Generally, we have to do very little for your community. Anyway Doctor, I am pleased to see you recovering well. I will let you know when I can come to visit your home. We have all your contact details and you will be hearing from us soon."

I was amazed at her total understanding of my illness and social condition and a concrete plan of how she and her team can integrate into my convalescence time with the support I may have from my family, friends and the community at large. This was health care at its pinnacle. She left with a smile of greeting.

By this time it was 4 p.m. and tea time in the ward. They had already taken my tea-time preference: small salmon and roast chicken sandwiches and English tea, which I normally avoid because of mandatory mixing with milk, which I can't tolerate. I started to take black coffee, even when I was a trainee in England. At that time it was a rare commodity to acquire.

But English tea in Canada—no problem, happy to be served anytime anywhere. I had my afternoon tea and was trying to settle down for a couple of hours when my visitors started to come.

Anyway, another ritual to fit into today's plan. I was already informed by the sister in charge to expect a visit by an occupational therapist to help me so I could return to my profession and the workforce. I knew not so soon, having seen the prolonged convalescence period after cardiac surgeries many I knew professionally and others socially.

Around 6 p.m. Mrs. Benjamin came to visit and introduced herself as the one would help me to return to work. Very pleasant, polite in her late forties, she asked me if she could sit down beside me to ask some questions about my work and what was short and long term plan to return to work. Again Mrs. Benjamin admitted that she was aware of my past affiliation with this hospital and the University. I told her my life story, and how I ended up in the cardiac ward.

"How interesting!" she said. She asked if I would like to return to my job, which I was doing.

I categorically said, "No, for sure, I am a clinician by hands and heart and a teacher in mind. Administration is certainly not my cup of tea, although for the last twenty-four years I have been at the helm of several setups of all sizes and functions in various geographical regions, I suppose I did my job well, otherwise I could not have stuck to the operations for so long. But this time as I feel fit to return to work, my choice will be to return to real medicine and not 'Paper Medicine' anymore," I told her.

Her comment was, "In that case let us make every effort to help you to return to work. Yours is a hard one, both physically and mentally, to administer. Before we return to work, our priority at present is to make you fit to get back to work. Our main problem with activities is protection of both scars. Although the chest incision is internally sutured with the metal wires and very difficult to break, if it does, all heavens will break, chaos and disaster will follow; even death might happen."

"So we need a full safeguard and security from the chest wound breaking down. We need similar care to the stomach wound. Jolting, heavy lifting, heaving, sneezing or coughing—avoid crowds who are not respectful to others with a physical disability. At the same time we encourage you to move around as much as possible. So to protect yourself from any collision, we advocate that you walk with a small pillow held on your chest so that any impact can be buffered. It will be odd to carry around in or outside the house. Not necessarily a small pillow, but any soft cushion or stuffed animal can do the job well. The benefits far outweigh the inconvenience. You will get used to it."

"We also suggest that you keep your bowels soft and going; constipation may lead to over bearing of abdominal and pelvic muscles, which will increase pressure inside your chest and abdomen, may be strong enough to cause rupture of the sutures. This is an unlikely event, but I must inform you of all possibilities. Any significant jerky movement should be avoided. I am sure you are well aware of these little but important care you need to take over next few weeks."

"I am not discouraging you from being active; on the contrary, remain active as much as your condition can support. You will be the best judge. Going up and down the stairs is encouraged, but initially take one step at a time."

In the next few days, she promised to visit me at home; that way she would be in the best position to assess and advise. "I will contact you well ahead of time. I am informed that you have a split level house. We need to work around this to make you most comfortable at home."

She bid goodbye and left.

There was another round of medication. The nurse left it in a small paper cup on my night table and said, "These you need to take a half hour before your dinner. I will bring one more, which you will have to take one hour after dinner. Please do not forget to take these now." She left. Now I had breathing time to look around.

My old roommate from the pre-operative ward was my new roommate now, after his valve operation. He had the same surgeon who did mine. He volunteered that his surgery was delayed by two days, because the anesthetist was not happy. Anyway, this is his second day in the ward. They kept him in the ICU only for a day and assuming he was well enough, he was sent to the post-operative ward yesterday. It is too early, as far he is concerned, and to think which way it will go. He has all kinds of gadgets around his bed, some attached to him, others are, I guess, in waiting. I thought there were a few more than I had in my first two days here. He was in a jovial and cheerful mood, although the results of the valve operation were quite a bit worse, than bypass surgery, at that point in time. I guess he had a very large family: sons and daughters, grandsons and granddaughters and a recent addition of a great-granddaughter. All came to see and pray for their dad, granddad/ great-granddad/ cousins/ grand-cousin's and so on.

The ward did not allow more than two visitors at a time, so it took several hours. A host of grandsons were there to assist in boosting Grandpa's morale and to pray for his quick recovery. Later I saw a Rabbi come to see him just as a friend, not to perform any religious rites. They seemed to be a very devoted and close-knit family.

To my surprise, he said he is lucky, that he did not have to go for a second surgery as I did. I guess the message was passed to his relatives by mine, since they had on several occasions met at the ward waiting room and exchanged the progress of their patients and their own anxieties.

Thank goodness, I did weather the surgeries well, praise the Lord, my surgeon, his team and all the staff looking after me.

In the meantime my wife came with her home-cooked dinner for me with her brother and sister-in-law. Both travelled from London to give moral and physical support to my wife in these stressful days. Friends and well-wishers also started to trickle in. I was able to maintain my humor to keep everyone at ease. I was showered with cards for well wishes and quick recovery and bouquets of flowers.

By eight in the evening, the room was empty of guests but for the occasional in and out of nurses, checking on their patients. I had been drinking all kinds of fluids, as advised. Now I got results. I wanted to pass urine. A nurse had to escort me to the wash room. Unfortunately, I could not. I was worried that they might have to catheterize me again. Then the nurse turned the sink tap on and said that this works sometimes.

It indeed worked. But passing urine became an agony, as if someone was slicing inside my urinary passage. Urine color was hazy and it smelt a bit. I thought it must be the result of last night's exercise. The nurse asked me to save a urine sample, for the doctor to see. They were going to call the resident-on-call now for advice.

Within minutes the resident was there. He examined me. I did not have any fever; there was some pain and tenderness in my lower abdomen. He said, he felt that I had developed a urinary bladder infection, whatever the cause might be. He would send my urine sample for testing, but he did not want to wait for the results. He wanted to put me on antibiotics against most likely causes of bladder infection. He did what he said he would do. I kept drinking in sips as I tolerated.

Throughout the night, I went to pass urine six or seven times. I had the urge, very little urine came but whatever the quantity was it burned my urinary passage like hell. I guess this was a double whammy effect of the urinary tract infection and the trauma caused by catheter manipulation.

I passed the night hoping and praying that the antibiotics will work and the discomfort will go away.

By 6 a.m., the painful micturition started to ease off but was still very unpleasant. This was after just the second dose of the antibiotics. By seven the new batch of ward staff took over. A gentleman nurse again woke me up. "It is 7 a.m., Doc. I would like to give you a towel wash and get you ready for the day's activities. Sorry about your cystitis. I hope it will get better soon."

"I hope so too!" said I, and let him carry on with his chore, that is, to give me a towel wash.

Then came breakfast. No toast, instead rice pancakes. I was impressed. I thought to myself, hope this is a "policy changing" move, not just for me. The slow dietary intolerance is mostly hidden, unrecognized and undertreated, resulting in various chronic illnesses, including bowel, blood and bone diseases. Diets are linked to cancer and heart diseases, the two biggest killers in general worldwide.

CHAPTER 17: In the ward (3)

I went to pass urine in the morning after breakfast. The pain was easing off. I was not frightened to pass urine any more.

At around 9 a.m., my old friend the physiotherapist showed up. She was in a very happy and cheerful mood. She asked if I felt up to walking with her today.

"Absolutely, yes," I said.

"That is a good sport," said Tina, my physiotherapist trainer. She went out to discuss with the head nurse if it was OK to start my physio-lesson now. She returned cheerful and said, "Let us go. You have been on bed-rest for so long, you will find some difficulty in maintaining balance while walking. But I will be with you; in case of real giddiness, I will support you and let you sit on the nearest available seat. Let us plan this way. We will go back and forth the entire corridor five times. Time is not important, but repetition and practice is. You will walk with me for the first lap and I will walk with you for the fifth and last lap. Gradually we will make you independent. You need to practice this as often you can, while you are in the hospital. This is an important step to be safely independent."

We started our walk with Tina supporting me. Indeed I felt giddy and slightly nauseated and short of breath as we finished our first lap walking the entire length of the ward corridor. She let me rest for a couple of minutes on a chair. Then we started again, and again. By the time I was doing my fifth lap, she was close but behind me. I still had some symptoms, which I could easily handle. Symptoms did get better with walking. She did say I could do as many times and as often I want, but to be cautious about any of the symptoms, chest pain and shortness of breath, and do not overdo it. I did not see any reason why I couldn't return to work soon.

"My next training will be to walk with you two flights of stairs, and check how much you can do. I will do it tomorrow. Their plan was to discharge you tomorrow, but likely it will be delayed by a day. The doctors will tell you about their plan. Ok sir, I will see you tomorrow more or less at the same time for walking the flights." She left.

At around 10 a.m., the medical team arrived. Quickly the Senior Medical Officer informed me about all my data from the screen, which was pleasing to them. They asked about my symptoms. "Tired," I said. "Mentally not as agile as I should be. My urinary symptoms are still there, but I am managing. Urine is clear, no blood clots in it but it is still painful when I am trying to pass urine. I had a satisfactory bowel movement."

"We are still waiting for your urine culture and antibiotic sensitive bugs; you might have an infection not sensitive to the antibiotics we prescribed empirically (our best judgment). But the fact your symptoms are easing off and the urine is clear tells me a different story. Our plan was to discharge you today but we thought we will discharge you home tomorrow. This will give our physiotherapist extra time to train you and give instructions for practicing some basic exercises at home. Should you wish to go home today, we can also make arrangements so that our team can coordinate with the home care team to provide you whatever support you need at home."

"I am easy, but I will take your suggestion to be discharged home tomorrow, if it is OK with you," said I.

"We are delighted; this way we can handle our entire plan in a systematic way without rushing it through." As they were leaving a young lady entered with a piece of paper and handed it to the senior medical officer, who did all the talking. He looked at the paper for a minute or so, came close to me and said, "This is your culture report. You indeed have a bacterial urinary infection; fortunately, both of the offending bacteria are sensitive to the antibiotics we have prescribed. You will continue to take the same antibiotics for the next four days. That is great," he said. "Keep well and I will see you again tomorrow."

The ward round with me went on a little longer than it usually does. I saw Tina my physiotherapist waiting just outside the door. She carried a small pillow, same size as a sofa cushion. I was not sure whether that was a part of my program or for her entertainment.

She was as happy and as jovial as always. "Well, I am happy to know that you decided to go home tomorrow. I have some time to spend with you about your physiotherapy program." She took out a file with instructions for twelve to fourteen different stretching exercises printed, with accompanying diagrams. She said, "This is our post-operative physiotherapy program. I will demonstrate each of them before I take you for walking the stairs."

Indeed, she demonstrated each of the exercises, one by one, and asked me if I followed her instruction. I did indeed. Then she said, "I will visit you at home, to observe how you are getting on at home without an instructor and continuing with the recommended exercises. Now, let us get on with climbing the stairs. This you might find a little difficult. You may be short of breath climbing the steps. But we can stop any time, if you feel the need to rest. This is the pillow I want you to hold against your chest while doing the stairs—for that matter always, while you are walking, or climbing the stairs, at home or outside for next month or so."

We started to walk to the staircase at the end of the corridor. I clenched the pillow in front of my chest, reasonably tight. She kept warning me, "Not too tight; it is just a support for your chest which is continuing to move with respiration, so that these movements, also, sneezing, coughing, sudden jolting so that the scar of the wound of heart operation may not be subject to excessive pressure from inside outwards, and get looser the metal sutures become unstable."

As I stepped up on the second step, I was giddy and Tina had to hold me. As I started to climb up, I was getting short of breath. After two more steps I was out of breath. I had to stop; I could not climb higher.

Tina said, "It is normal; as you go up and up, repeat these exercises. You will tolerate better and eventually will get used to it or the symptoms will gradually ease off."

Two more steps up. The central chest pain and that of shortness of breath was worse. I had to take rest, gradually after slow climbing, I made the first staircase. Now we were ready to go up to the next floor by slow climbing on the second staircase. The shortness of breath was serious, but Tina kept a close eye on my vital signs and did not seem to be much perturbed. She was also carrying "Nitro-Spray", in case should develop real angina. My agonizing distress seems to be a sign of her success, that she was able to make me climb up to the next floor and was able to escort me down to my room and then on to my bed, still panting, with moderate chest pain. She had to place the "Nitro" spray under my tongue once to help me breathe better and to ease my chest pain. The fact that she was able to bring me back to my room and on my bed was a sign of "mission accomplished". "This is normal," she said. "See if you can do it once or twice before you go home, so that we know you are competent and compliant to all the exercises, including the stairs. You have an advantage, that you have a split level house, your steps are ideal for our 'climbing the stairs' exercise. This is one of the most important exercises you will do to bring your heart back to normal. Also, we will make arrangements with one of the re-fit centers that is most convenient to you to train you for next three months as a part of our recovery program. I will give you all the paperwork to start your post-convalescence physiotherapy soon.

With her usual smile and good wishes she departed.

The next day at 7 a.m., as usual the male nurse woke me up: Good morning, sir!" he said. "It is 7 a.m., time for your wash up and get ready for breakfast. You will be going home today; we must make you as fit as possible." He gave me a towel bath on my bed. I even shaved, which I had not done from the day of my surgery. I brushed my teeth and got ready for my breakfast then walking in the corridor of the ward; climbing the stairs would follow, if I felt well enough to do it.

One nurse came with my medications and said, "These in the pink cup, you must take at least 15 minutes before your breakfast, and the ones in the white cup you need to take a half hour after your breakfast. You know the routine. We will explain the medications you need to take home and continue there, before you leave the hospital."

At around 10 a.m. the medical team arrived. They were in good spirits and a sporty mood. The senior resident asked me about my bowels and urine. I told him I was completely relieved from painful urination I did not wake up even once to pass water. I had normal bowel action this morning. I slept well last night and had my "a la carte" breakfast this morning. He checked all the data in the monitor and seemed to be pleased. Then he gently disconnected me from all my umbilical wireless attachments to the external monitors. I indeed felt free. I felt I could breathe better, although there was no reason to feel that way.

Then he examined my abdomen and chest, listened to my breathing, felt my legs and felt my pulse and took my blood pressure, with a blood pressure machine, just to make sure what is being recorded on the monitor is actually what is happening in my body, although the monitor recordings are all in real time and in real life. I liked his conviction that machines can't be trusted always. Human faculties need to be overseeing the mechanical functions and steer it clear from erroneous performances. Interestingly, machines can't think and detect and fix their mistakes. This may be changing to some extent. But as far as I am concerned I respect my God-given faculties over the rule of machines and their overpowering influence on medical practice and human life. There is nothing wrong to make machines work for humans, but there is everything wrong when humans work for machines. We lose our faculties and the vestiges of millions of years of evolution. We as human beings will be irrelevant. Only the machines, the machine makers and people keeping the machines and its makers alive (financing corporations) will matter. But their time will also come. The Frankenstein of

Machines and technology they created will not spare them either. When the machines and technology have turned our beautiful Earth to a Martian landscape, the machines will fall into their own trap. Nothing to do, nowhere to go, and no one to look after them, they will also rot in their own cocoon.

Happily I looked at the senior resident, with hope and aspiration, thinking that we humans deserve a much better future than what is almost about to befall us.

He said, "You may prepare to leave whenever you are ready. I will prepare your discharge note and send one to your family physician. Medications and directions will also be prepared. Normally we give two weeks supply of medications. We will make an appointment with your family doctor for two weeks from now. The social worker, the physiotherapist, the occupational therapist and the dietician will visit you within the next week for a long term domiciliary plan to organize your lifestyle that is best suited for you. One of the pharmacists will come to check on your prescriptions, to make sure everything is in order and you understood the directions correctly." Then he smiled and said, "I have to tell you all these as per our policy, but I do believe that you do not need this education; if there is something you can tell us to improve our services and approach, we will be hugely grateful." He mentioned to expect the consultant cardiologist to visit later this morning, just to check that every aspect is in order and you are fit and ready to go home. More or less a collegial courtesy visit.

Soon afterward the pharmacist and my cardiologist friend appeared at the same time. We had some simple chit-chat with the cardiologist. I was very grateful that he made time to visit me. The pharmacist went through the list of medications, doses, timings and duration with me.

Another lady entered, who appeared to be the ward manager, and asked if arrangements had been made for my pick-up from the hospital or if she needed to book a transport for me. I said, "My wife will be able to drive me home. She has made arrangements for me to stay in the main floor until I am strong enough to do the stairs to the bedrooms in the second floor." "That is fine she," said and departed.

The pharmacist and my cardiology friend also left, wishing me well and a quick recovery. The cardiologist said he would make an appointment for me to see him in a couple of weeks. His secretary will call me with the exact time and date.

It was lunch time. My wife brought a home-cooked lunch, to be consumed in the hospital for the last time, she hoped.

While I was having lunch, the ward sister came with a bag full of items they took away from me for safekeeping. She asked my wife if perhaps she would like to check the items. I could change into my clothes, if I wanted, leaving hospital items behind.

I heard a knock at the door. It was my family physician. I was pleasantly surprised to see him. A very busy family physician spared the time to visit a patient he sent for admission and treatment. I thanked him for coming. I said, "I have been discharged and will be going home this afternoon."

"That is why I thought to pay a visit to see your progress. Last time when I came to see you, you were in the ICU, under heavy sedation, just the day after your second surgery. I just received the fax from the hospital. He said that you have recovered well and will be discharged from the Cardiac post-operative ward this afternoon."

I was overwhelmed by his concern, generosity and professionalism. He also offered to drive me home, if I wanted. I said, "My wife will drive me home." I expressed my sincere joy and happiness for his generosity.

After a bit more chat on my recovery experience, he seemed to be essentially happy and bid goodbye.

As we were preparing to leave, I looked at my roommate's bed. The bed was there, but missing the person. I knew he had been transferred to ICU, because of fever and very low blood pressure, which they thought was most likely due to infection of his grafted valve. It was not rejection but infection of the grafted valve. This is not common, but does happen. Sometimes the valve needs to be removed and re-implantation of a new valve is needed. I would not know if he needed a new valve placement. But I was sorry not to see him and his usual humorous mood. I did not have the heart to think what might have happened to him, what events might follow. My few days' association with him before the surgery and also a couple of days after surgery in this ward was interesting and enlightening. He retired from the University as the Chairman of Economics a couple of decades ago, yet remained very active academically as advisor, planner, and reviewer for several national and international bodies and author of his vision on the new economy and those countries vigorously perusing the changing playing field, a hobby which he still pursued.

In a piece of paper, I wrote my best wishes and get well message for him and gave it to the ward sister to deliver it to him. I was not fortunate enough to avoid a second operation; I hoped he would not have to go through the experience of a second surgery for the distress which he might encounter, along with his family.

By 4 p.m. we were ready to move. A nurse came with a wheelchair. My wife grabbed the bag while one helper from the ward accompanied me and my escorts to the main entrance of the hospital. On our way out of the ward, I met several people— the nurses, young doctors other staff—who bid farewell to us and wished me a speedy recovery. A bouquet of flowers was also presented to me. I am not sure where it came from, will never know, but I was indeed leaving the ward with a sense of extreme gratitude and affection. I did wish for all patients who come to this ward to leave with a sense of fulfillment, as I am leaving.

My wife drove the car close to the curb of the main entrance. The nurse and the helper assisted me and my wife to get into the car and put all my belongings into the trunk. The nurse gave a big hug to me and my wife and waited for the car to slowly drive out of the hospital main gate, while they were waving at us, until we were out of their sight. We drove away slowly along the main road toward our home.

We reached home safely. A friend and his wife were waiting for us in the driveway to help us to get into the house and onto my place on the main floor. This little walk was so strenuous, with shortness of breath, chest pain and giddiness. Every step was a challenge; every step was a "step backward" to the grim days of sickness. I took one step at a time. I stopped a couple of times. I had to spray "Nitro" to get my breath back and ease the chest pain. Eventually I made it. I wondered if ever I would be back strolling on our street, walking the mall, going places which I loved so dearly? I had difficulty in imagining it. At least now, I did not see any light.

I was slowly settling down. I could not be more grateful to our friends and especially to my wife at this moment in my life. Life seems to be abandoning me. I never thought life would ever abandon me. I have yet so much to do, so much to give, so much to see. Can I ever get there? Life is so bitter. I thought it was my physical discomfort making me feel more despondent than what I should be for the illness. Actually it is the post-operative convalescence from a very major surgery, not one, but two within a space of 24 hours. For recovery, it is still very early days. As days go by I will get better, feel better and back to my wishes. I can't struggle with the feeling any more. I feel exhausted, tired, depressed. So I gave in and took shelter in deep sleep until the next morning, when my wife woke me up for medications. The dosages I missed last night can't be repeated today. I had my medications as prescribed and fell into deep sleep again.

Around mid-day I woke up to a strange voice. "Doctor! Doctor! Time to get up and get ready for your physiotherapy." That was my family physician. I slept for nearly 24 hours, without food or drink, and my medication schedules were all messed up. My wife got anxious and spoke to him about my deep sleep. He volunteered to come home to check upon me. He found me stable and had no reason to take any other action, but continued all the instructions I had from the hospital. We both were reassured. He left, promising to call the next day.

I did feel better after almost 24 hours of rest and wished to follow all the instructions as ordered by the hospital. I was still very tired indeed but more rational thinking kept me motivated to go along with life and take a day at a time. Why should I take the trouble? Will I make it? What difference will it make? What is the purpose? My feelings are still shrouded in grey clouds.

CHAPTER 18: Road to rehab

I am glad to be back at home. I feel released and relieved from a parade ground, but now, it is my job to keep the marching orders in order, for my benefit. I keep it; I get what I want. I neglect it; the road will be ugly, unruly, dark and bumpy. I got used to wake up at 7 a.m. The next day I was up by 7 a.m. and ready for my next routine. The previous night my wife sorted out the medications to be taken before breakfast and after breakfast and timely throughout the day in separate pill wells. I went to the washroom on my own. It was still difficult due to shortness of breath and chest pain and giddiness; they were all there, but tolerable. I did hold the pillow tight on my chest while walking inside or outside. This gave me such a sense of security and comfort I could not understand how could I live rest of my life without it. I could not even conceive what might be a suitable replacement, should I need to go outside to walk, for a chore or even walk to the pharmacy. The sense of security and subdued impact on my chest with each step I took to walk forward, or sneeze or cough—an added benefit was the warmth it retained on my chest, which was also highly addictive, pleasant and comforting.

I was wondering if I have to walk on streets, in malls and go shopping or for that matter, walk for any reason out on the street, what will the onlookers think? How will I feel walking holding a pillow on my chest? Never mind, I said to myself. *I am safe and comfortable; that is what matters most.*

On the first day at home I had all conveniences on the same floor. I did not have to climb a flight or go a down a floor to go to the washroom or take a bath. But from the second day, I had to start being mobile in my house, climbing or go down at least half a staircase (as my house is split level), I had the advantage of making it to the next level using only half a staircase. In fact, that was the case during my training at the hospital. In spite of fewer steps, it was a deeply distressing, uncomfortable and painful experience, which is difficult to forget. Memories are still raw. I dreaded to make any attempt to go above the stairs to next floor for wash up or use the washroom.

In the morning, all my medications were organized as per timing, before and after breakfast, at lunch time and at bedtime, etc. After I had my breakfast, I was contemplating going to the next floor for cleanup. Contemplating and contemplating, but I lacked the spirit to take the plunge. My wife came to help. No help — this is another dose of treatment ordered by doctors at the hospital: an attempt to climb up and down the staircase two to three times a day, and increase as my tolerance improves. I got up, picked up my pillow, held it against my chest and started to walk towards the staircase. I felt giddy and did not feel that I could make it up to the staircase. I took a deep breath and started to walk slowly; every step forward was a challenge. Unsteady gait and shortness of breath were the main obstacles. With the help of my wife, I made up to the staircase. Now came the acid test.

The first step up was tiring but I managed to overcome the distress. As I climbed the second step, I started to feel short of breath. I did not dare to make another step upwards. Shortness of breath, palpitation and giddiness all regained control over me, in spite of my spirit and desire to overcome them. I lacked energy and any enthusiasm to pursue further. This would be a breach of doctor's orders. My wife came and helped me to push me to go up one step at a time. I had no time to think or feel what was going on. By the time I climbed 6 steps to the landing above, the whole world was going in circles around me; I could not see what was in front of me. I was so very short of breath that I felt I was drowning. I have a morbid fear of drowning, since I can't swim. Now the fear of really feeling of lack of oxygen in my lung was overwhelming. I was feeling choked, unable to breathe. Maybe I am going to lose consciousness. I am still standing, can hear and see what is going on around me, but barely. I have the feeling that someone is splitting my chest again. The pain was so sharp and agonizing and unreal, I thought I had gone out of this real world. Dead? No, in that case, how come I am so aware of my feelings and what is happening around me?

I was about to fall (or sit on the floor) when my wife squirted some medication in my mouth. Nitro-spray I guess. Within seconds, I gained my faculties to some extent. I felt that I was able to breathe, the drowning feeling was gone, giddiness was slowly tampering down, and the chest pain was eased off. So is the power of a single squirt of "Nitro". I can hardly dare to go without it carrying with me. I was able to wash myself, brush and shave, being fully conscious, but tired, very tired indeed, as if all my muscles needed rejuvenating. I had no idea, how I could do it. But life has to go on. I was aware that the effect of Nitro would wear off in a couple of hours. I may have to keep spraying, as I go along, to keep living at a level with the feeling life is still worth living. I slowly climbed down to my bed on the main floor. Back to my comfortable cocoon.

At around 11 a.m. my family physician called to check on how I am faring at home. He promised to visit at the end of the day, see how he could be helpful for faster convalescence and other recovery plans.

At around 11:30, the Social Worker called, requesting permission to visit me at home, since she was in the neighborhood. If it was not a convenient time she would make another time to come. My wife answered the call. I told her to come today, so that I would have an idea about her observations and suggestions. She said, she would be there in half an hour.

She had a good understanding about our social environment. She looked around, went to visit all the floors, the rooms, the washrooms, the kitchen. She said, "You have such a big house, but it does not give the feeling of emptiness like many other I have seen. Every floor has its own character and charisma to itself." Anyway, since my wife is the only caretaker at home most of the time, she suggested someone to come to help us with shopping, getting the medication from the pharmacy or any other chores outside or inside. She may even help us do some cooking and cleaning. I did not object. It is better to have someone from the establishment, rather than one from the agencies. Unfortunately our experience with agency-sponsored workers in the past on several occasions had been less than satisfactory, if not disappointing. With this arrangement, she left. She left her contact details and said if we were not happy with the services the helper was likely to provide to call her and she would get a replacement. Or we could call her for any problems, if she can be helpful otherwise. This is routine provision for the health care system.

I am still struggling with my mobility and shortness of breath and chest pain. I can walk on the same floor a few steps, then I need to rest. Maybe I was expecting faster recovery. Climbing above the stairs is still a nightmare to me. But I must go on, if I am to get back on my feet and try to live a more or less normal life. So I tried to go on the steps of the staircase. After two steps, I was unable to climb further; giddiness and fear of falling prevented me. As I tried to go another step up, I would have fallen had my wife not come to assist me to prevent a disaster. Then again she pushed me above slowly, one step at a time, as my shortness of breath and chest pain was getting worse. She sprayed one squirt of Nitro again in my mouth, under the tongue. I did recover and climbed down slowly, still panting and clutching to my pillow on my chest. I decided at least for the next couple of days, I would not attempt climbing up the stairs unless I had help to do the exercise. It can be dangerous. Or disastrous. One of the main duties of the helper lady had been to walk me up and down the stairs, when she arrived and again just before she left.

At around 4 p.m. my GP knocked at the door. He indeed came as he promised. We were so very happy see him. He checked my pulse and listened to my chest. He made me walk up and down the stairs and checked me again. He was able to witness my distress for the exercise. I thought I would get comfort from his observations and let me go slow.

On the contrary, he said, "You are doing well, considering it is just about a week since a very major cardiac surgery. Do not let it loose. Use the Nitro with caution." But I can use as often as I feel, while I am active. The only problem is giddiness and unsteadiness, which I need to watch. He also suggested that from next day, I must start walking in the park to improve my rate of recovery. He did not anticipate any risk. He volunteered to come and walk with me in the park for first couple of days, until I felt confident enough to do it myself, but someone would need to accompany me for next few weeks. We were very pleased indeed for his professional and at the same time friendly concern. He left leaving a very positive vibe, which was difficult to create on my own.

After my Doctor left, we sat and as per permission from my cardiologist, I was allowed two cups of coffee per day. So with my habit of an Englishman's afternoon tea, I was allowed to have light black coffee with special biscuits and my wife her chosen tea and biscuits, to ponder on the past and the way things might come in the near and not-so-far distant future and strategize how to cope with the present situation. We agreed that I must start the plan to walk out in the park from tomorrow at least once daily. I could not have even imagined how an adult male can walk in public places clutching a pillow on my chest without being embarrassed or being ashamed, putting mildly my emotion for the exercise.

A little later the phone rang. It was Tina, my physiotherapist from the hospital. She wanted to know if she could visit us tomorrow to set me up for my physiotherapy programs. We agreed that she could come at 11 a.m. That was the plan. She hung up with assurance for tomorrow's visit.

"I call him religious who understands the suffering of others."
- Mahatma Gandhi.

CHAPTER 19: Rehab arrangements

Aside from medical treatments, exercise plans and programs, I still had been promised by the dietician and the occupational therapist to discuss their plan and advice for my quick recovery. Indeed, at around 10 a.m., as we had just finished our breakfast, the dietician called, and having asked about my progress, wanted to know what will be the best day and time for her to see me and discuss the diets, if we wish. I said, "Of course, we will be pleased if you can make time tomorrow to come, perhaps some time in the morning." We agreed and she was pleased to be able to advise us on my diet and dietary needs the next day.

The day was rolling along. I did my steps on the stairs once. Still not easy. Chest pain, shortness of breath and giddiness still bothered me. I had to sit down on the top of the staircase to take one spray of Nitro. That eased off the symptoms to some extent. I have been doing only half of the staircase climbing all this time. I felt I could give a try to complete the other half. I called my wife to stay with me for my next adventure. She was ready and willing with the "nitro spray" and the small portable oxygen cylinder loaned to us by the hospital, courtesy of the social worker. I did not have to use it so far but completing my climb to the top of the staircase, felt like competing with Sir Edmond to climb the top of Everest. I might need the help of the gift from the social worker, should I run out of breath and if help from the "Nitro squirt" can't completely give me enough relief and energy.

So we started to climb the other half of the staircase, one step at a time, stop and take a deep breath and release. I continued my climb after I had the fifth step out of eight. My panting, shortness of breath and loss of balance did scare my helper, who suggested that we call it a day for this exercise, rest for five minutes and then climb down (which was not easy either). I said, "Yes." I rested a bit, but did not get down; I climbed up to the top of the stair. Catching my breath, still hungry for air, for a change I could feel my heart was pounding. Gradually, the giddiness and nauseous feeling became less and less. I was ready to stand up and start climbing the stairs again. That is what I did. Slowly but steadily I negotiated one step at a time and eventually, got up the stairs. By the time I got there, I thought I would collapse and that would be the end of all the trials, tribulations, pain and suffering of thirteen hours of difficult surgery.

As I got up, I felt feelings of accomplishment, success and joy. Where is Tenzing; where is Sir Edmond? Please wish me well. To my utter surprise and failure of a Doctor's (that is mine) prediction, I had no added symptoms or discomfort, no more than what I had at the beginning of this last lap. I sat down for few minutes and contemplated whether climbing down two half flights at one go is a good idea or do one half at a time. I started one by one and climbed down the first half. Since I had no extra symptoms, I thought I would continue, knowing my wife was with me with all her aids in hand.

I made it to the bottom of the stairs and to my bed. I can't say it was an easy climb down. I was sobbing, clutching hard to my pillow, breathing hard too, but did not feel faint or nauseous.

Maybe this is the beginning of my getting better. If I can do these stairs at home, a few days after a major surgery, I will be able to do it anywhere soon enough. We are expecting Tina the physiotherapist's visit soon.

She indeed turned up on time, with her instruction manuals and some tools of her trade, actually a bunch of rubber tubing. We sat down and chatted a bit about my experience at the hospital. Then we narrated as detailed we could my last few days at home. I was happy to tell her my achievement to climb up and down the stair today and completed the mission; as she explained, climbing up and down the stairs will be my most important "road to be fit" again.

She was very happy to hear, but cautioned that I must do it with help around for next few days and not try on my own. It is still very early days for the body to make a major adjustment to progress toward "great again". But I will do it; most people in my condition do it, especially the surgical team who work with me. Then she was taken for a tour of our home, looked at all facilities, stairs, steps, washrooms, kitchen and access to the garage, etc.

Then we went through the expected routine of several exercises I am to carry out for the next six months. Interestingly she also commented our home is a good tool for my getting better. Being split level with four separate stories, I have no choice but stay active, just to continue my daily living. She advised that I move up to an upstairs bedroom and make sure I keep taking all my medications. She will arrange with one of the "Re-Fit" centers, where heart patients are referred for three months of post-operative rehabilitation program, where they will train and teach me essential exercises and advise about several aspects of "lifestyle change" to adjust to my new physiological environment. The first three months are part of the health care post-cardiac surgery rehabilitation program. She suggested that it would be a good idea to continue with the program on my own expense for another three to six months, not covered by the Health insurance. These were her recommendations, but it certainly was my personal choice to follow it through. She strongly suggested following the plan.

The Cardiac rehabilitation center will call me with an appointment. She will request them to start my program within next three to four weeks, no later. She left with a promise to keep in touch and will be happy to help me any way she can.

I am yet to see the occupational therapist, who will be visiting the next day. The nutrition advisor will also call sometimes next week.

It seems slowly but surely we are making progress. I started to feel optimistic; perhaps a bit of encouragement from Tina and a definite plan of action for recovery gave me the air of optimism. Either way I am feeling good and ready for the next challenge.

The next challenge is to relocate me to my bedroom another half story above. The scenario changed within next half hour. As soon as the order came from the physiotherapist, my wife got to work and made my bedroom patient-friendly and convenient; at the same time my main floor cocoon was also dismantled to make it look like a lounge again, where I can mingle with my friends and visitors as before, should any one choose to visit. There was no dearth of well-wishers to give me company, friends and those who had gone through the same procedure and recovered. Some of them were back to their normal work. One of them was an airline pilot. Was he flying another Boeing 747 or a 380? I never dared to ask. A few of my physician colleagues also went through the process. Their experience and helpful suggestions were invaluable to maintain my high morale and look forward to an active future.

The day ended well.

The next day by 10 a.m. the occupational therapist arrived, a very energetic experienced middle-aged lady. She asked about last few days since I returned from the hospital. I narrated everything I had to Tina and was also proud to repeat my excursion to the second floor yesterday, which I had repeated this morning, prior to her arrival, with difficulty, but it seems to be easier every day. She wanted to know apart from my personal care, how much she was expected to do—cooking, cleaning, washing, shopping, etc. I did tell her I do not need to do any of the chores if I choose not to. But I will help my wife with whatever is allowed and I am capable of. Moreover the social worker, Susan had arranged to send a home help for the next two weeks starting tomorrow.

That is great. Needless to say any heavy lifting or sudden jerky activities, I need to avoid for the next two to three months. She said, "You had a very active and busy professional life. Now is the time to take it slow but not stop."

Then she took a tour around the house. She was pleased with the bathrooms which needed no modification to accommodate my revised life style. The split level build of the house is good for my recovery. Normally there is no real restriction for driving, but that advice need to come from my cardiologist. Generally patients feel well enough to drive two to three weeks after the surgery. I suggest waiting until you have the first post-operative checkup by your cardiologist. In the meantime, transportation can be arranged for essential activities, i.e., doctor's appointment, hospital or pharmacy visit. If no other help is available transportation may be provided for essential shopping, etc. It was very generous of the health care system, but I said for the time being, until I get the green light from my cardiologist, my wife will be my driver. Should I get stuck, I will contact her for assistance. Then she asked how I would spend my time when I am not carrying out the plan per doctor's orders. Then we went to look at my office along with my personal library. I had everything in my personal office at home that I can ever expect to have in my work office.

This is where I spend my time while I am not at work or not sleeping. "

I bet you do!" she said. "If I have the kind of life style you do, I would do the same. How much time do you spend every day for watching TV?" she asked.

"That is my least priority during my waking time. I leave it for others to do."

"You have a large flat screen TV in your office?" she asked.

"That is for conferences or for any educational event. The TV in the basement, where I rarely go, is used for entertainment."

"That is good! TVs are not good for rehabilitation time after heart surgery, both from a physical and mental health point of view." Some will say it is debatable. But I agreed with her.

As she was assured that my mobility remained unimpaired, activities and house work plans were all acceptable for the duration essential to recover. My return to work would be advised and discussed with all physicians concerned in the next six months or so.

Any problem I encounter in my daily activities, personally or ergonomically, institutionally or bureaucratically, I am to let her know and she will do whatever way she can help. With assurances of "keeping in touch" she departed happily.

By this time it was lunch time. The doorbell rang, and waiting outside was the social worker with another lady, the home help she promised. She introduced her as June, who had been assigned to help us for the next two weeks. She would help with chores inside the house, cleaning, cooking, assisting with bathing if needed, answering the phones, doorbell, shopping and picking up prescriptions, etc. June had been helping people at home now for more than ten years. You just tell her at what time you expect her to start and she will leave when we are happy that she might finish for the day. "I am happy to help any time you need, just call my number." After a few health questions, the social worker left.

June is around her mid-forties, happy, energetic, and willing to start doing something as soon as possible. She asked my wife what she would like her to do.

"Thanks June," said my wife. "We have been so busy just keeping up with all the requirements for the patient, I had no time to vacuum the house. I know this house has several half floors and a basement for living; if you are feeling energetic enough, would you like to do the vacuuming? You need not do the entire house today; you may do one or two floors a day. That will be quite acceptable."

"Thank you," said June. Without further ado, she went straight down to the basement and picked up the vacuum, checked the ins-and-outs of the machine, joined it with the outlet and switched on the power, and there started to vacuum from the basement slowly up the stairs to the next floor and the floor above. She finished the entire house in just over two hours. With the ease and sense of familiarity, she did her job, it felt as if she lived in this house. She is familiar with every nook and corner, every crack and every bubble and bald patches in the wall.

For next fifteen days June was an angel, helping physically, amusing us mentally, and expressing concern about our families living far away from us. She did have to pick up long distance calls from various members of my family, close or distant, friends or acquaintances. She did the job very well. Her help was invaluable; her compassion and empathy did fill up some of the vacuum left behind by departed family members. Beyond her job as home help, she did help me to walk in the back garden. The first time it was difficult, very difficult indeed. I wished my wife was with me with the Nitro spray and portable oxygen cylinder. I had difficulty in understanding why it was difficult with giddiness mostly, shortness of breath and severe muscle ache. I wish I had not come. I guess all those times I was active in my own air-conditioned cocoon, the difference in air temperature, humidity and possibly some inherent fear of "if something goes wrong" mostly influenced my exacerbated symptoms during my first stride outside the house. A few steps and several deep breaths later, I started to feel better, as if I could match the effort of our adventurous home help June.

She confided that she had taken care of several heart patients at their home. Generally they are not difficult to handle. But people who had knee operations had been most difficult to take care of. Although she is not expected to do any personal care, there is no escape if one is at home with the patient, walking the patient, changing the bed sheets if they get wet and if no other caregiver is available in short order.

Trying to being helpful and being helpful from the inner core of the heart with empathy does not come easily. One must feel lucky if one gets one home help with the latter qualities. That is what June was. In two weeks, she totally enchanted us with her help, concern and friendship.

Nice words aside, we could not have been more grateful to the social worker and June being so humanly helpful during our time of distress and uncertainties. She was overtly missed as she completed her assignment and moved onto her next patient.

Although I am doing my best to stay mobile, it is nowhere near the normal requirement for activities for an average person; on the other hand, at present I am not an average person nor is this an average time. Yet we realize that I need to improve my mobility, to return to a reasonable physiological state.

It is not a problem of passing urine this time; it is extreme constipation that started to bloat my abdomen. It is just bloating and an increasing feeling of bloating. I did speak to my GP. His suggestion that we approach this therapeutically means taking aperients, laxatives, enemas, etc. Once my bowels are open and active, then dietary and focus on activities will be on order.

So we followed his suggested plan of action. In two days my bowels were as regular as can be. We concluded that it is lack of mobility that is likely to be the one major contributor to uncomfortable constipation. Resuming a more active life than I can tolerate, that is, my heart and body can tolerate can't be forced. Having discussed with my cardiologist and GP, we agreed that a cautious combination of medical treatment and physiotherapy including walking will be best approach toward faster healing. They also cautioned that my tolerance is my judgment, particularly as far as exercise and walking is concerned. But they encouraged me to push little harder as days go by. They also emphasized that my planned post-operative physiotherapy need to start by three to five weeks from my surgery. The physiotherapist may be able to set an appointment with the cardiac rehabilitation center. But until then continue to remain active and follow the stretching techniques Tina has taught me as often as I can tolerate.

The next day, having spoken to my cardiologist and GP and asked we could walk along the driveway and the road, we ventured to give it a try.

I held my pillow the physiotherapist loaned me and a walker. But I could not use it because I needed my both hands to clutch the pillow on my chest. So with my wife's support we started to walk along the driveway. The driveway is inclined slightly downhill.

For the first time coming outside the house, clutching a pillow on my chest felt funny and embarrassing to some extent. It was morning. Most people on my street have left for work.

Children have already gone to school. The road is practically empty except the occasional car passing by. Coming downhill on the driveway was not so difficult, but by the end of it, as we hit the main road, my giddiness and shortness of breath started to be obvious and uncomfortable. My wife gave me a squirt of Nitro and within seconds, I felt better and started to walk. Slowly but surely we made our 50 yards of walking exercise and returned to the house. I had to have one spray of Nitro on our way home. By the time I reached home, though my shortness of breath and giddiness were better, but unpleasant generalized muscle ache was so intense that I could not reach my bed and sat on the floor for few minutes and returned to my bed with a big sigh of relief.

I spoke to my GP about my first experience in outdoor walking. He suggested since walking on the street can be risky; accidents and falls may result in serious injury, I should start regular walking exercise around a duck pond in our neighboring park. My GP volunteered to accompany me for first time to go to the park. He will come with me for first couple of days, just to give me moral support. I was delighted to have his company for my first adventure outside.

CHAPTER 20: Active physiotherapy begins

My memory of my first experience with walking around the duck pond is frightening. But perseverance and persistence got me over the initially depressing mood. My GP's assurance to lead me on to the circumvention of the duck pond was inspirational, but knowing how busy family physicians are, I did not feel desperate at his absence. My best care taker was with me; that was my wife.

We drove as close to the duck pond as we could. Then clutching my pillow, I started to walk. It is no more than a 20-30 feet walk. By the time we walked to the pond I was all puffed up and wanted to sit down. My whole body was aching like hell. I was not able to walk straight, because of dizziness. I had my magic potion, the Nitro spray. The action is instantaneous. I started to feel better. I wondered if nitro also had any psychotropic effect. Anyway my guardian angel let me sit on the bench to catch my breath.

The duck pond is an oval pond, with several benches along the side of the paved walk that encircles the pond, placed at regular distances; maybe there are fifty of them around the pond. I noticed many men and women, both old and grown-ups, walking alone, some in pairs, some families pushing prams. My immediate impression is that aside from the ducks in the pond being attraction, circumvention of the pond alone is a popular destination, for pleasure, for amusement of kids and most importantly to retain and regain one's health. I never knew the duck pond is a prescription item for practicing doctors. People running, marching, striding along, strolling at ease, walking with canes, walking with walkers or being carried by a wheelchair—an incredible scene. I never knew such a place existed in my city. All these activities along the side of the duck pond may be inspirational and motivating to the weak and infirm, but the sight of so many people trying to get back to life and living may be disheartening to others. But I am energized.

Everyone had a reason to be there: pleasure, relaxing, staying fit, getting better, hoping to get better, and connecting with God, entertaining, family or friends. Some people may not have any reason, that is, the reason "to have no reason" is their reason they are there, not empty but expanding to eternity, without a goal— what a wonderful feeling of absolute freedom that might be. It is difficult to imagine or even perceive to all "goal" seekers. Unfortunately or fortunately, I am one of the goal seekers; that is why I am here.

I got up feeling perfectly fine and strode gently forward. By the time I arrived at third bench, I did not think I could do it anymore. I had to sit down to rest. After five minutes of rest, I got up and felt confident to walk and started to march forward. Alas! By the time we reached the next bench, I had all the symptoms of climbing up the stair: giddy, shortness of breath, chest pain, nauseous feeling. I had the second squirt of Nitro. My wife thought this is the time to quit today. We will try again tomorrow. There are about fifty benches around the pond; I could barely do four today. Will I ever be able to get to the fiftieth? Not at this rate. I did feel dejected to some extent. But looking forward, I tried to convince myself, this is day "one". I have time to catch up. Staring at several people strolling along the bank of the duck pond, certainly some of them had my "day one" feeling. They have succeeded, they have completed circumvention of the pond not only once a day or maybe twice or more. The good thing is one can measure success by counting the number of benches one can cover in one attempt or how long it takes to circumvent once or how many times one can in one day. All these are measurable to monitor one's progress and success.

That may be the reason why people return here again and again; that is why I will be back again tomorrow.

In the meantime timely medications, from before and after breakfast till before bedtime, went on like clockwork. Diets as advised and regular stair climbing with whatever stretching exercises I could do at home continued. I had no choice but to follow the orders executed by my guardian angel. I started to feel more and more confident day by day at home, but outside was a different ball game.

We returned to the duck pond the next day. Walking from the parking area to the pond was just as difficult as yesterday. I had to take rest on the first bench. I was short of breath and giddy. I had to have one puff of Nitro. I felt better. I started to stroll slowly toward the second bench, then to the third, then to the fourth. I felt I needed to rest. I sat down and took several deep breaths. Gradually my uneasiness started to improve. I did not think I really needed the second puff of Nitro. I strode slowly to the fifth bench and my symptoms returned again. I rested on the fifth bench. No Nitro puff, but longer resting time and more deep breaths. After 10 minutes or so, I felt I could return slowly to the car. That is what I did. Today was a day of progress and success. I had only single puff of Nitro and I advanced to the fifth bench. I was not overtly joyful, but not depressed due to slow progress. Slow indeed; progress nevertheless.

I returned home. A few friends came to visit. They were encouraged listening to my story and the progress I made at the duck pond.

As days went by, I conquered one to three benches at a time. It was not easy. It was trying. It was scary at times. But I did it and over a course of twelve days I was able to completely circumvent the entire duck pond with or without my Nitro puffs.

Then I continued to circle around the pond, from one circle to two circles to three circles (with difficulty) and got more and more confident in my ability to be independent and return to a normal life. That was still a dream, but I did not give up.

My appointment for the rehab center came. The next step of action toward recovery was to follow the rehab program advised by the experts.

"Everything has beauty but not everyone sees it."
- Confucius.

CHAPTER 21: Rehab and recovery

Depression is hardly in my vocabulary. I took a photograph of a very dark cloud in the Libyan sky (while I was in Libya under Col. Gaddafi; how appropriate that photograph was in Libyan life, now living at a distance and looking into the past, I can appreciate that photograph's relevance) with a very thin silver lining on top of it. I cherished that photograph, framed it and hung it in my office to remind myself that every cloud, no matter how dark it is, has a silver lining—no matter how slim it is, a silver lining nevertheless.

As for every human being, life offers ups and downs, peaks and troughs, exuberance and desperation. As a human being I am no exception. But depression spares me or I may have some strength to ward off depression. Since my surgery, I could really feel at times deep depression, at times suicidal for no reason. Although I know well the surgery has been a success and I am progressing slowly but surely toward returning to normal life, yet the last drop of zest for life and building a new beginning after the heart operation has eluded me. I know I need to do significant adjustment in my lifestyle, my routine, my likes and dislikes, my passions and my aversions; people who have gone through this process kept reminding me time and again. Lack of energy is understandable, but the lack of zest for life, even to dream of a beautiful, happy future, comes as a nightmare.

Eventually I had to settle, these are only thoughts and passing thoughts, far from reality. I had to forcefully convince myself that these are not my thoughts, coming not from heaven but from hell. Like a painful tooth or severe attack of asthma, we need to live it out and can't dwell on it. But during the attack, life is unbearable; there is no time to think of quiet time and smooth sailing when these attacks are gone. They do. But post-heart surgery-induced deep, unbearable depression hardly gave any reason to feel that light is round the corner, the sun will be rising again at dawn and there will be light and happiness soon. Now there is gloom everywhere, and pining for the dawn to break. But that is not in my hand so I continued to live amidst a dark cloud, where the silver lining is hard to see.

The plan to attend today's introductory session at the Rehab center should elicit a great excitement, but that is not the case. I have very little enthusiasm nor any desire to do anything more than what I am doing at home or I am able to do at home. This total apathy, I kept to myself. I did not express it to my wife.

When the time came to get into the car to drive to the center, I started to have chest symptoms, shortness of breath, giddiness and nausea at a lower scale. I had not done any extra physical effort to account for the sudden appearance of symptoms. I convinced myself they were most likely psychological, which may or may not have a physical factor. I expanded this logic to my depression, apathy, lack of energy — to more psychological than physical factors. Just the positive reasoning started to make me feel better and in a barely positive mood.

It was a cold winter day, late in the morning, when we set out for our first appointment at the rehab center, which is just about twenty minutes' drive from my home. My wife drove me to the center. My appointment was at 11 a.m. We reported to the reception. They were expecting me. The receptionist asked us to wait in the lounge. Soon Mrs. Nancy Temple, our nurse chaperone, arrived. She remembered me well from work at the hospital. She was keen to let me know the reasons for her to switch from a very busy clinical nursing practice to a more or less passive clinical public relations job. It was mainly to be able to give better attention to her two young children. At the same time she did get the scope of educating patients about the practice of rehab offered at the center. The majority of cardiac patients do not have a clue about the "rehab" program, what it entails, its importance for recovery and return to active life. It also educate patients on various exercise plans and the scope of activities offered by the center: physical, psychological, lifestyle changes, etc. Interactive didactic classes are offered on various topics. Some of them are part of my comprehensive package; others I need to purchase tickets for some seminars.

Then Mrs. Temple walked us through the entire facility. It was amazing, organized, huge, equipped with all forms of instruments for exercise, running and walking tracks, and even a secure place for a bonfire. She took us through the cafeteria. I was quite elaborate, with plenty of space, both for sitting and an area for small, intimate parties. Big screen TVs piped music and film. In a lecture theatre, we saw someone busy with her lectures with the healing seekers.

There is a small theatre, where students are discussing the topic of presentation. The whole set-up did not look like a playing field, but that of a university building. Educating to stay fit, to stay happy, to stay productive, most importantly to stay connected with compatriot health seekers, family, friends and many colleague in and out of work, neighbors or casual acquaintances, to expand our horizon of community.

Everyone feels part of the big family making the journey forward.

Technologically the center is fully equipped if not overtly equipped with the most modern body building, body shaping and healing machines. There is ample space for everything. The walking or running track is close to half a mile with four well-defined tracks for use at various levels and for various ages.

Just the physical set-up and various activities energized me. The depressive mood slowly started to wane, yet it had not completely disowned me. I was still uncertain of my life and existence. Where I am going? What next and on and on.

This is however the physical introduction. The Program has not begun yet. Waiting eagerly for events to come.

Mrs. Temple took us to a separate room where a few others were waiting for the introductory rundown of the entire exercise, educational, dietary advice, lifestyle changing events and plans. After her session, she asked if my wife would be joining with me for my rehab program. The center encourages a partner to participate in the activities. According to their experience, particularly for cardiac rehabilitation, patients with an active supporting partner do better and recover faster to normal life than one without a partner. And for the first three months it is free.

So my wife had every reason to participate with me, especially now it is the winter months. Nancy took us to the floor and started the first stretching exercises. We both followed her religiously. It took just one hour to demonstrate and us to practice the exercises. Then she walked with us on the track and explained the rules of using the track in a disciplined manner, so that there is no clash between users of differing levels and objectives.

She advised that we must try to come at least three times per week, then gradually increase it to five and then to daily activities. She also promised she would accompany us during our initial training from the instructor. There may be ten to fifteen people training in one group, but the space is adequate for everyone. She also said there are six levels of various exercises to be done and in six weeks all will be completed. We can repeat every program on our own, if we wish, daily after the training. An instructor will be available to help if needed.

There are several water fountains inside, scattered throughout the arena. There are also bottled water dispensers available, should we wish to purchase the water. Having given us a comprehensive picture, both physical and programmatic, she introduced us to several instructors. It was time for Nancy to say goodbye with an appointment for tomorrow to start my rehab program.

"Educating mind without educating the heart is no education at all."
- Aristotle.

CHAPTER 22: Rehab program continues

The introduction to the rehab center and the program had been quite illuminating. We felt confident, knowledgeable and remained hopeful that the program offered will take me to the path of complete recovery and back to my normal active professional life, which I missed so much.

Every day with my group of "aspirants", I religiously attended our training. Every week we graduated from the training and went forward to the next step and next emotional fix.

I continued to have shortness of breath. My instructor would allow me to take a pause, catch my breath and continue with the exercise. I experienced the same symptoms while walking the track. I felt giddy and occasionally off balance. For the first week Nancy would walk with us and instruct us to take a pause or drink a sip of water, rest for couple of minutes and then continue on.

As time passed my tolerance to exercise and ability to walk without a pause improved. Two weeks into the program, I was able to catch up with other fellow team members without any pause; at times I outperformed them. Nancy was pleased to see the progress and improvements in my vital signs, which she had been monitoring at regular intervals.

Thus I continued for three months, adding more and more cardiac exercises and walking faster and faster around the track—in general getting closer to my normal shape, both physically and mentally.

The rehab center is a whole world in itself, containing human beings like a huge extended family whose only goal is to return to normal life. In this community I was surprised to see so many of my prominent professional friends and associates as neighbors at the center. They all are there for a reason. A few come regularly to stay in shape. The majority had cardiac surgery of some sort and is in a rehab program.

Whenever I get time, I stop one of them and ask about their health, work, their family and progress with recovery and the impact of this program on their recovery. Most of them are coping well with their personal and family issues. For one of my professional colleagues, who was obese to start with, both he and his wife had bypass surgery almost at the same time. That is sad and troublesome. His children generally live away from home. One daughter had to give up her job to look after her parents. There had to be a major social adjustment. There are financial pressures, yet they seem to be happy in the way things are moving along. The daughter accompanies them to rehab on their scheduled days. They have home help, yet much responsibility lies on the daughter, who also has to look after two small kids of her own. They have taken the situation in their stride and are carrying out living as normally as they can under the circumstances.

Another friend of mine, a university professor, seemed to be overjoyed at seeing me on the rink. He looked well. He has been on the program for over six months. He greeted me saying, "Welcome to the club. You need to have a couple of bypasses, or your valve yanked away before you can join this elite club of intellectual-fortunate or powerful politicians like American presidents or so." Stress is certainly a common factor for these people. But I could not justify that stress had any major contribution for my cardiac ailments.

While discussing with my knowledgeable physician friends and other cardiac scientists, I discovered people of my ethnicity, that is, of East Indian origin, do have a shortage of Vitamin B6, which apparently causes shrinkage of the muscles of blood vessels, which fails to pump blood forward, results in stagnation and causes deprivation of oxygen in the heart muscle, giving angina and heart attacks. I am not certain how established this theory is in the medical scientific community, but I am relieved that it is unlikely that stress had much to do with my heart condition or there may be another viable reason for me to have an acute heart attack other than stress.

For the next six months, I followed meticulously whatever I was asked to do. I made sure I walked the rink at least once when I visited the center. I started with a quarter of a circle in the beginning, stopped due to shortness of breath, then slowly progressed to a full circle . By the time my six months was over, I was able to circle three times without having to stop or being short of breath.

One does not make many friends on the track. Everyone on the track is trying to reach their goal; some of them are struggling and others are at ease. Yet we got to speak to few, those who walked with same speed as mine. Little "hellos" continued afterwards in the center's cafeteria one floor above. The staff interaction—some very complimentary, some good, others not so helpful—generally all complimented the general high standard of both professional and support staff. Eventually a few went beyond the Center, into the beginning of their illness: how much they had to suffer, the long waiting list, eventual coming of "D" day, experience at the hospital, family members' support or lack of it, coping with the long post-operative recovery period. One person said she was sick ten to fifteen years ago, or she would have been better off both physically and financially. Of course divulgence of personal issues was not common, but people did from time to time, not necessarily out of desperation but to share with an equal sufferer. We did make some long-term friends, from entirely different social, professional and cultural backgrounds.

At the cafeteria some people are easy to chat with, while others need a little extra mile to bring them out of their cocoon, and understandably so.

But some of my friends who are here for the same reason also wanted to know my experience and progress. We did exchange our mutual agony and aspiration. Most of us would like to return to work; some can't wait while others had enough; spend rest of life in Southern states, the Caribbean or spend time with family and grandchildren. Others wish to spend as much time as one can cruising around the world; others still want to travel, as long as their hips and bones cooperate. It was a very revealing cross section of people's attitudes and impacts from heart operations.

There in the center we attended several seminars. One of them was given by a clinical psychologist from the university hospital. It was specially focused for all patients attending following heart surgery. There were about twenty (20) of us in the group from all professions and all levels of social strata and religious beliefs.

He wasted no time in announcing that this is one of his most interesting and challenging groups. He said, "We have four doctors, one pediatrician, one rheumatologist, one oncologist and one gastroenterologist, as well as one university Professor, one CEO of a national insurance company, two engineers and one newspaper editor. I had never been so lucky to be associated with such a wide variety of 'illuminates'. I hope to tell you what I know and expect to learn from you all gentlemen, and address the questions and confusions I might cause."

I do not know if this was a psychological approach to bring the entire group together around him. However, he seemed to be an extremely humble individual. That put all of us at ease.

Amongst many psychological conditions associated with heart disease, for that matter any serious illness, he emphasized the most common psychological presentation is "Depression". Most of the patients complained that they are depressed. The majority of a patient's depression can be explained due to physiological changes, changes due to the illness, what he described as pathophysiology, while others can't be explained with our current knowledge about depression itself. He admitted that purely psychological phenomena associated with heart disease and related treatments including surgery do exist. Of course we have started to understand the neuro-biological pathway to various psychological and psychiatric phenomena, but the unknown is immeasurably vast, the researchers' eternal playing field. The thick wall between psychology and neurology is crushing the barrier between psychiatrist and neurologist is slowly disappearing as we start to understand various psychological phenomena and psychological diseases, their neurological and physiological connections.

One interesting issue he brought up about mentorship and mentoring, why to some people mentoring and mentorship works like a charm. The influence of mentors can be life changing. Yet there is no drug, no medication no ECT (electro-convulsive -therapy, a common technique used for treatment for several psychiatric illnesses), but it does work. It works because the "Mentees" made it work, through their neuro-biological input.

In the end he also mentioned about the neuro-biological effect of meditation, yoga, Tai chi, prayers and even chanting; he expects they work through our neuro-biological activities. To support his assumption, he did mention works of several famous scientists, worldwide.

Aside from several practical tips, in concluding remarks he gave us some understanding how to ward off fear and uncertainties, not only for the period of convalescence, but for the rest of our lives. He also said, "Now that we know that we can heal ourselves better than the greatest healer on earth, we ourselves are in charge. What he has done is to put gas in the tank of our Ferrari or the Humvee or Volkswagen Beetle."

For more than an hour he kept us spellbound, one of the best presentations I have heard on the topic. That in itself is 'therapeutic' enough, far more worth the time we spent. The post-presentation period was short. He had to run back to his class at the university. He promised to continue interaction, as we wanted.

Subsequently, we had presentations, educational seminars on diet, healthy lifestyle, life-long engagement, family life and an interesting topic on sexuality of patients with heart disease and after heart surgery. That seminar was overflowing, with both patients and spouses and some health care workers.

The presenter was a lady nurse, apparently with years of experience as a nursing teacher and educator. She has been giving this lecture at the rehab center for several years and it remains as popular as ever. One can surmise just by seeing the crowd of thirty-eight to forty in a room with chairs for twenty people. Several were standing against the wall; others were sitting on the floor. The pressure must be high enough on the administration to let so many people cram in one room. Maybe this is a onetime special occasion.

She is a no-nonsense lady. Her first question was addressed to the entire group: "How many of you speak to your spouse or partner about your sexuality and sexual feelings?" After one minute of pause, since no one raised hands; she said, "Indeed I did expect this silence. This is a difficult issue to talk to others, even your spouse, whatever the reason might be. We frequently inspect our feelings; even that introspection not infrequently becomes hazy and unclear, without any clear understanding of our own sexuality," she said. She continued, "My main audience is patients with heart condition or who had recent heart surgery or their spouses." She apologized that she must focus only on this group.

"To these groups, I must emphasize that they must accept the fact that their cardiac illness did impact significantly on their general health, activities and performance, both physical and mental, which includes their sexuality. There is no escape from the feelings of being sexually incompetent. That is why it is important to speak to close and intimate family members and best friends. Particularly patients who are recovering from a heart attack or recovering from heart surgery need to understand that unlike any other surgery or illness, recovery from heart attack or surgery takes a longer time to heal. So the course of building up intimacy with sexual partners needs to be slow, progressive and strong.

"Once one is ready for sexual activity, we need to understand that physical exertion for sexual performance may be as much as climbing full sets of stairs or a brisk walk for 10- 15 minutes. However if one gets short of breath, must stop physical activity, including sexual activities, and report it to your doctor. Eating heavy meals and drinking alcohol just before sexual activity poses higher risk for induction of a fresh heart attack."

To be able to minimize the effect of the risks for recurrent heart attacks, she suggested, that one should keep an open eye to every individual event not acceptable for normal activities. Patients should communicate to friends, neighbors, and family as often as practical. They should stay fit, exercise, and meditate to improve mental and physical activities.

She also emphasized to look good, use cosmetics, smart not expensive clothes but with good taste. We had a program for terminally ill patients to look good, feel good, and get better faster. An improvement of self-image must impact on a patient's psyche, through their neuro-biology feedback, that makes them feel well as they look well.

There is no alternative to stay fit by regular exercise; whatever is tolerable to the individual to improve one's sexuality.

She spoke well and took the time to respond to some useful and some not so useful questions and queries. I felt at the end the attendees were reasonably content and informed of sex and sexual activities, relations and intimacy with their partners.

We made several friends with staff and patients over the six-month period. The routine had gotten into our system. I did not think that we would stop the program abruptly. We had developed a new but beneficial lifestyle. We would continue, especially since I do not have to wake up every day at 6 a.m. to be at work by 8 a.m. At least I will have a reason to go on living and look for a brighter, more active and productive future.

At the end of months, I went through a rigorous physical examination, lab tests, x-rays and scans to find the progress and ability to be active in my profession. The doctor who examined me was an internist in a hospital five minutes from my house. He knew me by name and was happy to see me and also seeing the progress, he said I could start to think of going to full time work. I will be able to do it. It will take some readjustment in lifestyle, which will impact my revived physiology. He did not anticipate much problem, but said I am my best guide. Stop when my body says to stop.

He said, the report will go to both my family physician and cardiologist. Between them they will work out the medical regimen I must follow. Until I see them I need to continue what I have been ordered by the hospital at the time of discharge. But while I am still a client of the rehab center, he will continue to monitor my progress and work in liaison with my family physician and cardiologist.

"What we know is a drop, what we do not know is an ocean."
- Isaac Newton.

CHAPTER 23: Return to work: a million questions

I think I am better, or I am getting better. My doctor said that I am fit to resume my work. I had a very busy life almost from the time I qualified as a doctor. Aside from my personal duties as a junior doctor, I was too happy to stand in for any of my colleagues who needed help, to cover for them day or night. Staying busy, just not busy but doing something worthwhile is what I hankered for. Hours of the clock had very little meaning to me. My last job with an international organization needed huge amount of travelling and flying, spending time in the airports. It was impossible to organize my day, to plan a plan. The plan was that there is no plan, only issues to attend to.

Now I feel it was a blessing that I got sick and was grounded for a very long time out of my schedules, my routine, rounds, clinics, research, presenting, publishing, teaching and directing research, all almost at the same time. I loved the life I had, but my family did not. But I had unquestioned and unwavering support from them.

Now I did not know what to do with my forced unemployment. I could not think; how could I return to a busy clinical and leadership position? Am I employable? If at all what position might I be offered? Will any institute or organization employ me, knowing, I am at a risk of serious cardiac condition? Can they rely on me to discharge my responsibilities? Can I still be a team player? Will they take advantage of my vulnerability and try to buy my services cheap? Even with my outstanding credentials, when the question of dollars and dimes comes, dimes come as the first offer. Particularly private corporations lack a sense of decency and respect for human beings and contributions to the profession, when dollars and dimes are the issue.

Do I really need a job? I know I will not be starving, but I know I have still lot to give to the profession. I would like to work with a team, with colleagues, which I have done ever since I qualified. I perform better in a collegial environment. I need challenges and I am never shy of challenging. I have evolved in adversity. I play well in adverse environments. That is why I need a job.

I can start my own practice. I can join with my brother in his health care facility. But as I started to look for a suitable job the real world did show its colors. Health condition, age, out of practice—all these kinds of excuses and reasons were given for being rejected. Organizations which I would not have even talked for employment, even if they came with a golden bouquet, I would have gracefully rejected. However at this time, even those people, those organizations, either do not respond to my email, do not return my call, or discourteously fail to acknowledge my thirty-six page thick Curriculum Vitae, with some internationally famous personalities as my references.

This was very depressing. Rejection from my own profession and professional organizations and institutes, was deeply hurtful. As time passed, I started to feel useless, empty, and at times suicidal in a semantic sense. I kept trying. I wanted to start teaching in my home university. That did not work either, because they felt uncertain about my performance. Moreover, like anywhere, one needs to be born in the inner circle; it is impossible to break through the circle, to get a niche for oneself and succeed. Well-wishers abound, but tons and tons of wishes, does not translate into real employment and breaking the circle to gain access.

I continued to contact medical institutes, medical schools, research centers, pharmaceutical companies, government bodies — I did not leave any stone unturned. I knew one of these days my problem would be answered. I know I can survive without a job; my family will not starve, and I still have a decent life. But the total and absolute neglect, disrespect, not recognizing my ability, was the main source of annoyance and shame on my part. How much insult one can take? Moreover, these people were ignoring my applications and my capability.

A break came on a Saturday morning, a phone call from one of my old friends from England. He said, "I understand you are looking for a teaching faculty position. We are the largest medical school in the Western Hemisphere and I am the chairman of the Department of Medicine." He would like to invite me to visit his department and the medical school. He had a few professorial positions vacant. If I was interested, I could come down just for a visit and then decide what I prefer to do and what is available there.

I could not have been any more delighted. It just so happened that next week I was going to Miami to attend a meeting. We arranged to fly from Miami to Dominica.

I arrived there next morning. The school's transport and the "meet & greet" lady were present. We drove from the airport to the campus through the winding mountainous roads lined by tropical forest, banana vines, coconut and palm trees, huge evergreen trees, bushes and shrubs. After one hour of adventure-drive we arrived at the campus and then to the Guest Hotel.

At around 2 p.m. my friend arrived with another faculty member. We chatted a bit and planned to visit the campus next morning.

Next morning, one of the faculty members came to pick me up. We went to meet the Chairman in his office. Inside the campus, it is a complete story, North American ambience. Very different from the natural scene we saw en route to the campus from the airport.

My friend introduced me to various faculty members, other chairs and the Dean. Having discussions in depth and my medical history, we agreed to start as a visiting professor two to three weeks per semester, which might increase as needed and eventually a tenured status. I was happy to be engaged and happy to be in an intellectual environment, with students and the opportunity to create my specialty in cooperation with the government hospital.

I started my new job the following month. From dejection to elation, it was a break I needed so badly. Rejection from institutes, academic and non-academic, big and small, almost pushed me to the brink of giving up and "ending life". But my life has a far greater, wider stage than to get a job. My family, my dreams were still alive, my friends and colleagues and the world at large, which I have cherished so much, differing, landscape, differing geography, culture, ethnicity, food, their history all had been fascinating to me. I have yet more to discover for myself and tell the stories. I am not yet ready to quit. Circumstances were making me to believe maybe I am a quitter.

Having being born and worked in an environment of secured job and a "Paycheck" at the end of the month takes away the spirit of adventurism. That is what was lacking. I have now the stability of a paid job and a paycheck at month's end is reassuring. Freelance entrepreneurship is yet to be attractive to me. Yet I like my personal freedom at work; fortunately, I was never deprived of it.

So far in my career, I did not need a break. In fact I have fixed broken organizations, fixed broken systems, restructured practice habits, patched up broken ideas and concepts. Now I needed a break desperately for myself to rejoin my broken career. I found it was not coming from all the sources I have tapped so far, until I got an early winter morning call from my friend. I can't ever forget his help to rebuild my morale and my career. The opportunity he created for me, the opportunity

I availed, gave me a platform far greater than he or even I thought.

In the past I had the opportunity of working with several "beautiful minds" institutes that outshine the brilliance of "God", countries with trillions of dollars to spend. I never failed to keep my promises to deliver even more than was expected of me. Now I have the opportunity and a complete, empty, barren platform, especially to practice my specialty. From an empty base, with blessings and well wishes from my associate and the authorities, it was possible to create from nothing an "Unimaginable something", well organized, well run and well-liked by people of the country, to help them with their illness, which could not have been treated at home in the country.

This was my frightening challenge, my worst nightmare and my best achievement. Skip hundreds of papers, books and chapters, spending night after night the in lab, getting students through, residents ready for life's challenge, all pales in front of my last act in an isolated part of the world, giving them the opportunity of treatment and hope of cure from cancer, at home, should they ever need it for them or one they love. That is my gratification.

I am thinking this may be the "silver lining" in the "dark cloud" of my cardiac surgery. There are not many. Here I count my blessings.

"Facts are many but truth is one."
                              - Tagore.

CHAPTER 24: Return to work: cash flow crunch

Without a job, without a paycheck, where will the money come from? Having lived with a lifestyle and social environment, the most important date in the calendar is 30th or 31st (29th Feb in a leap year), because these are the paydays, when our paychecks come to the bank. We all look forward to this day, rich or poor, manager or janitor, we are all in the same boat on this day. No check, no monthly groceries, no shopping, or going to the theatre, or walking by the beach with some snacks (peanuts preferred; they are cheap and in abundance).

In spite of the fact I do not have to have a job, I will still live, eat, sleep, go to the movies and vacation, like my family. I still miss a job and the paycheck at the end of the month. If I was in my forties, I would have plunged into freelance entrepreneurship, if I could not find a job which would satisfy my professional practice and needs, expose me to academic and intellectual challenges with colleague, give me the opportunity to work in a collegial and team environment. With the security of a paycheck at the end of the month, I can concentrate on my job and not counting dollars and dimes. Will that suffer?

I have a large extended family: brothers, sisters, cousins, nephews and nieces, uncles and aunties. Most live close by and one can reach each other by walking, driving, flying or on "whatapp". Within an hour, the entire clan can be seen and connected. That is our closeness. All are professionally successful and financially well-endowed and independent.

I have not stopped worrying about my personal fiscal stability. Concerned about financial turmoil in the world economy and what it might do to my personal money supply — if I am not around who will take care of my family? They will never seek help from relatives. Who will advise them the best way to deal with a financial crisis, if that does happen? Even if I am around a world economy downturn put so many people worldwide out of their houses, on the street, lining up at the food bank. Just unthinkable.

How much can we trust our financial institutes? How many Madoffs or Sanfords are out there is anyone's guess. These chilling thoughts made me seriously anxious and concerned about our financial stability. The chance is small that these events might affect us, nevertheless the chances are there. We have insurances of all shorts. Unfortunately companies are more concerned about the list of conditions for denying payments than legitimate reasons for payments. Recently I had to communicate with a health insurance agent for my coverage on the phone. I was concerned about the legitimacy of the contract. For reasons known to them, I did accept the condition and agreed to listen to her on the phone.

She reconfirmed my bio data and the medical history. The last part was conditions of payment. She read the conditions out loud to me. For nearly ten minutes she read the declaration. She went on and on, saying if this condition is not met your claim will be declined. For next ten long minutes all I could hear is that, "You claim will be declined… your claim will be declined… your claim will be declined… your claim will be declined… the decline announcements went on and on for ten minutes. Then I said, "Thank you madam, it would have been easier on you if you could tell me, maybe one word when my claim will be accepted instead of reciting for 10 long minutes. I can help you to rephrase your declaration; saying just one short sentence: we will do our best to decline your claim; if we fail only then we will consider your claim, after it has been scrutinized by three levels of review panels."

I know my close family will never have reason to ask for financial help from me. But who knows, if the world economy can create havoc for me, the chance that they will also be affected is high. How can I help them if I am out of job and without a paycheck? How can I help anybody financially, if someone needs help for some genuine reason, if I have no paycheck coming?

Very depressing and disheartening thoughts. But these thoughts continued to hound me, no matter how much psychologist or social worker counseling was made available for me.

The constant thought of financial instability, did never leave me, until I was well settled in my new post-heart surgery job in a medical school as a Professor.

"Compassion is a spiritual quality that is unique to mankind."
- Sikhism

CHAPTER 25: Rehab continues; millions of questions; family disruption

It is difficult to forget when my heart surgeon told my wife and rest of the family, that post-operatively I had a 50-50 chance for recovery. He confided later to me that he really said what he seriously meant. I did get over that crisis period. I am still around 10 years down the road. I guess all cardiac surgery patients have to live the rest of their life with the Damocles' sword of a 50-50 chance of making it through. Today I am on the right side of the fifty–fifty chance; who knows, tomorrow it may be the wrong side. Then I am gone.

Since the surgery, although I have taken life as it came almost to a normal level, rarely do I think that a time will come when I will be not around due to natural cause of ageing or progression and recurrence of my heart condition. It is the fright of "not being around" that hounded me since I came out of the hospital. Yet generally I remain calm, get on with life's needs and demands and my fascination to remain clinically active as long as I can. The fear of my absence in my extended family, its repercussions never left me. The effect may be ripples or a tsunami, destabilizing our family our clan's stability.

We had some experience, when our brother at a very young age died in a traffic accident; the effect on our family dynamics was devastating, and not a ripple but the effect was that of a tsunami. He was an industrialist, doing very well in his business. He was very popular in the community. He kept binding all of us, looking after our paternal home, looking after our parents in their old age. Our family home was a magnet for all our brothers and sisters to congregate during their holidays; we will gather there from various cities and generally energize our kinder senses, and have a wonderful time together. Our father predeceased him. Mother was still alive; she had to bear the shock of the news of his violent accidental death.

Our paternal home was a large house, one of the iconic buildings of the city. He left an infant son and young wife behind. For a while my mother took charge. But the absence of my brother was so deep and so profound; my mother also passed away a couple of years later. Then all hell broke loose. There was no one young and responsible enough to maintain the big family home, to maintain its attraction for all of us to congregate. With time the building started to deteriorate. My oldest brother expressed his incapability of maintaining our paternal home and sold it off; we became rootless. It was very painful and disturbing. The spirit of our parents, our family cohesion, was devastated.

That is what happened when we lost one of our most loved and cherished brothers. The feelings are still clear and vivid in my mind, the gradual disintegration of family. We just not lost one brother, but lost the family bond we had for each other. I lived farthest from all. I could see the gradual disintegration of our brotherly affection. Just because we lost one. Had he been around, we still would have our family home, a physical focus for all like a honeycomb to honey bees.

I must say, our upbringing, our parents' love and affection helped us to bring all together again, though it took years to bridge the gaps. There was no rivalry, no animosity and no hatred. Just the physical separation; infrequent contacts led to the disintegration

While I was in hospital bed, at home recovering, I had nightmare from time to time about his death and the profound and devastating effect it had in the cohesion and strong bond we had amongst us. We are all self-sufficient; we do not depend on anyone for handouts. We all live comfortable lives. But his death set us apart in a passive manner. As we are growing older, we look at each other for more cohesion, affection, mutual support and closeness.

If it was completely in my hands, I would have not allowed another vacuum, due to my absence. The reality is that was not in my hands, not even in the hands of my doctors, who saved my life to start with from a devastating serious but silent heart attack. For ten years I lived with the fear of creating a vacuum of my absence, not for me, but for my close family, my brothers and sisters, and extended one. Just the thought concerns me; what I did notice happened after the death of my brother. I have gotten over my personal fear of death, but not the effect of my brother's death on the entire family and the dynamics of our life and existence.

CHAPTER 26: The rehabilitation: ten years down the road

It is approximately ten years ago I had the bypass. I have lived all these years under Damocles' sword of 50-50 chance to make it good. My surgeon saw me one month after the surgery. He never had to see me again from a surgical point. I met him a few times. Every time he has been happy to see me, to see that I am still on the good 50-50 side. We laughed and joked about his prediction. The good thing is that he cleverly did not give a time limit. I am also happy with it.

But I have been monitored every three to four months by my cardiologist and every so often by my family physician. I continued my rehab program for one year and gradually had to cut down the time due to lack of time and or lack of proper facility. My medical school had an excellent set up for fitness activities, with the most modern gadgets, machineries and very helpful and pleasant trainers and a big and spacious building, which automatically attracted me to maintain exercises as advised by the physiotherapists at the hospital. I feel fit. My cardiologist said apparently all my lab data, scans, x-rays, pulse and blood pressure are at healthy levels.

He restricted my fascination for "junk" food, reduced fat and sugar, and plenty of fluids daily. He ordered no more than two cups of coffee a day; that was a killer, but I gradually got used to it. I cleverly drink only one third of a cup at a time. That will give me "Six Coffee Kicks" a day; that is tolerable. There is a lot of psychological element to my "coffee fix", I realized. Aside coffee deprivation; regular planned exercise, at least half an hour of brisk (as tolerated) walking must be my daily mantra, he said.

I voluntarily reduced my meat intake, I do not seem to miss it. I do not mind simple boiled stuff for the time being. In spite of me being grown up in "Curry culture", I also had to dilute my cultural ethos and stand by what my dietician and my doctors said as an important aspect of the change in life.

For the first couple of months our preoccupation with following the doctor's orders got us busy and we had very little time for anything else. I did a bit of reading and my wife was absorbed with her crossword puzzles in whatever time we could snatch out of the new lifestyle and new adjustments. From time to time I was still walking with my beloved pillow, which was so comforting, consoling and invigorating, I had difficulty in weaning myself off the pillow over of my chest.

Eventually I did. But that pillow always stayed in the back seat of my car.

As exercise and routine visit to the rehab center became set in my daily routine, I had time to think what next. Other small things, small inconveniences, to which I did not give much attention started to crop up.

Surgery was not the end. Aside from the rehab program, I had to take multiple medications, some before breakfast, others after, some before lunch, others after, some in-between, others before dinner, others after, some before bedtime, some on an empty stomach, others with food, whatever permutations and combinations one can think of, I had gone through the years. They say there is no free lunch. The price of staying alive with supporting medication can be another interesting challenge embedded in the process. All medications have side effects, some are loud and others are quiet. For a few months into the rehab program, I noticed that I woke up in the morning with severe bone and muscle aches. Muscle pain frequently was so severe that I had difficulty in getting from bed. It is not only stiffness; I also had patches of muscle twitching, repeatedly so that I could not be walking, but would be in bed for a long time, till mid-day when I get a hot water bath, which takes ten to twenty minutes of time, to ease my muscles, joints and bone pain. I struggled to cope with the bone, joints and muscle pain. Hot bath, full body massage, muscle relaxants, all were tried and sometimes helped for a short time; others not. But I bit my teeth and clenched my jaw, trying to convince myself accepting these little in conveniences has a wider and brighter outcome, so I thought.

When the problem became critical, I went to see my cardiologist for help. He reassured me that this is a common side effect from almost all cholesterol reducing medicine. However the degree of reaction varies from person to person. Unfortunately my reaction is excessive. There is no point in continuing with same medication. He gave me another cholesterol reducing medicine. I returned home joyfully.

The reaction from the new medication was much less to start with. But as time went by the reactions slowly crept up. I maintained my part of warm bath massages, rolling from side to side on bed on floor carpeting, taking muscle relaxants and pain killers to ease the discomfort. It helped initially but their effects also wear off.

This is the nature of cholesterol reducing medications. Over the next two to three years, my cardiologist switched over to different cholesterol reducing drugs, as one became intolerable. Now we settled for on one for last three years, which is tolerable and managed to keep my cholesterol down. Significant progress has been made over the last ten years in medical treatment of heart disease; we expect to see better medicines with fewer side effects and improved control of cholesterol and cholesterol induced plaque.

At times I wonder, once I was told by doctors that we East Indians get heart disease not because of increased cholesterol in blood, but because of withering of thin muscle layers in small blood vessels, due to vitamin B6 deficiency, which fails to steer the blood into the heart muscle. In that case just a B6 supplement should be good enough. I hope we will know soon. For the time being, I guess doctors do not wish to introduce another complicating factor by withholding anti-cholesterol medications.

My cardiologist and my GP warned about various side effects to expect from all the medication I need to take postoperatively. They were right. While I was recovering, with the help of multiple medications, the side effects at times felt worse than the path to cure.

One particular medication or group of medications gave significant amount of phlegm with associated cough. Lung congestion did not help my shortness of breath. At times a persistent cough caused chest pain, especially on the scars from my surgery. This is a well-known phenomenon and remains a long term issue for most of the patients. Even ten years after my surgery, certain medications I need to take give me excessive phlegm and sputum.

Mostly it is clear, but production of phlegm does cause increase in coughing, shortness of breath due to congestion of the air sacs of the lung, and occasional chest infection – in my case more than average. This may be due to environmental factors. It may also partly be due to stunted immune system, resulting from a very major surgery. Immune system suppression after any surgery, major or minor is unavoidable. Sometimes the suppressive period can be months long, generally 3-4 weeks after surgery suppressed immunity recovers. That is why we are at a higher risk of getting infections of all kind, mostly treatable and completely cured.

Anyway the lucky ones sail through the reactions and side effects; some like myself have to pay for everything either by cash, credit or kind (just a semantic), before we thought we might regain our health.

For the first six months after the surgery with rehab plan and multiple medications on strict timing and strict regimen, dietary recommendation, is all for good, but it is not easy to maintain a disciplined life while one is going through the recovery process. Physical discomfort, socio-economic issues and psycho-social issues can be overwhelming. Healthcare support, guidance and a happy home are ever encouraging with a positive outlook; all come together to get us through the most trying six months after the surgery. You get better every day; every day is a new day. Climbing up the ladder is hard. You go one rung up you are marching forward, hard difficult, challenging, but progress nonetheless, look below and back, only full of painful memories. Don't look below or look back; dark memories will pull you down. At least that was the case for me.

The path of healing and recovery, as challenging as it is, also full of surprises. Sometimes I could see and read at a distance, which I could not do even when I am in my best form of health. I am quite shortsighted for a long time. I did not need to wear my glasses. This happy event stayed few weeks. Just as I was about to get used to not wearing my glasses, that little bit of good fortune left me in a hurry, in one morning. Nobody could tell me why it happened, how did it happen and why did it go away?

In another event about a year after my surgery, one morning I woke up and could not get up from the bed; the muscles of the backs of my both legs were completely paralyzed. I had sensation, but did not have any power to move. I had no fever, or any other symptoms, to justify the almost absolute loss of power. Only of the muscles of the leg on the back. I tried to get up and just slipped out of the bed on the floor. Could this be due to my extra enthusiasm for my "Rehab – routine"? Could this be due to side effects from the whole lots of drugs I am taking? This could be from one of them or mixture of them or for an entirely different reason. That was very scary.

I called my GP. He asked me if I had any problems with passing urine. This morning, I do not know, because I am still in bed. But last night I had none. He asked me to call an ambulance to take me to the ER. Otherwise, he will look in after his clinic is done by 3 p.m. I promised to call an ambulance to go to the nearest ER. Then I got out of the bed and slowly walked, supporting the bed, to the washroom. Plonked myself on the toilet and within minutes I had a complete clean out of both the bladder and the bowel. By this time my both legs started to twitch and then heavy shaking. I was really afraid. In two minutes the shaking stopped, and I was able to stand up and walk back to my bed. I thought I will give it a couple of hours before I call the Ambulance. I could not believe how fast I recovered from that life-threatening event. Next morning, I was in reasonable shape, better than before surgery.

Minor events of nausea, giddiness, thumping headache, photophobia (light sensitivity), lightheadedness, periodic insomnia and many other small but irritating symptoms continues to come even 10 years after the operation. Yet I am grateful for the second lease of life I got to spend with my family, friends, and pursuing my passion that is taking care of my family, my patients and my students.

En route to this journey to recovery, I met many people: my fellow sufferers, recoveries, sitting beside them in the Doctor's Chambers, hospital waiting rooms for tests and minor procedures, walking on the tracks of the rehab center or pulling the rubber bands for group exercise, attending educational seminars with fellow suffers or the ones who intend to protect them from suffering, meeting friends of friends at their houses while visiting socially. The cafeteria and the lounge of the rehab center seemed to be a wonderful place to introduce one to perfect strangers. The sources were huge and opportunities were enormous. I found it is easy for people to open up themselves, to a fellow sufferer even if he is a perfect stranger or even a doctor.

As I was regularly at the rehab center tracks, as per instruction, I came across many fellow walkers, some of them are running, others fast walking, some keeping up with me, others I even had to leave behind. Everybody takes their task seriously. Some have time and mind to wave at you, some say Hi, next day how is it going? The next step of being intimate, how long have you been coming here. I am here for last one year, they might volunteer the information with or without me asking, and that tells you that he wishes to exchange his experience with you and would also like to learn from me.

"How you make others feel about themselves says a lot about you."
                                                              - Islamic quote

CHAPTER 27: Learning from fellow stranger-sufferer

As I was tracking, a fellow tracker, tall, handsome and very healthy looking man, was walking at the same pace as me, coming regularly to the rehab center, he looked like that he is maintaining his health, not recovering it like myself. This is how our interaction started. For several days, we waved at each other. Then we graduated to "Hi" as we passed by each other, then, "How are things going?"

"Okay with me! How about you?" I said.   "Fine!" he responded. Then we continued to walk, he walked past me and that was the end of tracking that day.

Next day, I was late, he had the dosage of walking, and he was having his coffee or some sort of drink at the cafeteria on the second floor. I said hello to him and asked permission if I could join him for my drink. He was delighted. I took a seat and introduced myself, started talking about, how I landed up here, not that I regret having been here and spending my time.

He introduced himself; professionally, he is a chartered accountant, heading the firm's office in the city. He had chest pain, irregular pulse, fainting episodes for last two years. About four years ago, he was told sooner or later he will need replacement of one of his heart valves. He was managing with medications. But for last two years, his chest pain, palpitation. Fainting spells all increased. He had to take sick leave and leave of absence although he managed most of his work from home he said, but the situation was becoming untenable.

"About three months ago finally, I had my first heart valve replacement. That was a 6-hour surgery. I recovered fast and well. Two weeks after I returned home, I started to have fever, chest pain and palpitation. Doctors diagnosed that I have infection of the grafted valve. They gave me a course of antibiotics for three weeks. I felt better initially, but my chest pain and palpitation, shortness of breath, cough, all returned and was slowly getting worse.

"Eventually about six weeks ago, the surgeon decided to remove the infected valve and replace it with a new one. So they did. Six weeks ago I had new valve placed in. I had much better and quicker recovery and now I am on to my rehab program, getting better by the day. This rehab program has been wonderful for me." He also admitted by discussing with me of his illness, he feels relieved of all anxieties, many question he had in his mind unanswered also clarified by speaking to me. He had no idea that he would bump onto someone who can relieve anxiety without a prescription, but by some simple words.

This discussion went on for several days over the coffee table, I also narrated my story to him, at least it is of some consolation to him; he said that doctors do get sick and they do suffer like anybody else, And those who do indeed feel the pain, distress and sufferings like any other human being.

Another young man was in my exercise class. He was too young to be a heart patient. On the other hand who knows what might have happened, that he is forced to join our group, instead of going to a football match, hockey game or twiddling his thumbs on a smart phone watching some video game. This is the cherished life. One day after the class, as I went up to the cafeteria for a glass of cool healthy drink, I saw the young man also sitting alone, with a cup of coffee. He is barely in his late twenties or early thirties.

I greeted him and extended my hand of friendship. I introduced myself and took his permission to join him in coffee.

He is in his early thirties, spoke well and politely. He introduced himself and said he is apparently helping the family export and import business. He said that his family is from Iran and they have been in carpet business for generations. Recent political changes forced most of the family to escape and settle in North America. He is an MBA student at the university.

After that day we had several friendly chats. One day he asked me how I was doing, how the programs at rehab center helped me and if I had any cardiac problems. Then I volunteered about my condition, the treatment and management I was having at the hospital, at the clinic, has been excellent. "The rehab center's programs and help from the staff are all exemplary. At least that is what I feel. I hope your experience is the same. These people are always open to ideas."

"Oh yes! I like this place, a great one to forget the world and focus on yourself." He said as a child he was diagnosed to have Eisenmenger's syndrome. He had surgery for the illness in Teheran. He was well; he had several symptoms from fainting attacks to black out, palpitation, headache and chest congestion. "I used to be blue and pink. I had a flushed face all the time. The doctors in Teheran did diagnose the illness correctly and apparently a small surgery at the Tehran University hospital. That was about six years ago. We had to leave Iran five years ago and we settled mostly in Canada. But we still have a large clan back in Iran. Being Zoroastrians one is always under pressure for changes conforming to the wishes of the power.

"Anyway I still get occasional palpitations and chest pain. I have been seen by cardiologists. They have not detected any real problem. As part of my healthy living, I come regularly here to do some organized exercises, walking, etc. and attend seminars, which I find interesting. Although at the university we have a huge gym area with all available facilities, it is always crowded. We see all too energetic, enthusiastic and competitive people.

"Here the population is different. One gets energized seeing the life and energy of post-retirement group. People recovering from major heart, joint or nerve surgeries. Damaged body, damaged mind, damaged souls getting fixed, just by changing life style and changing the outlook on life. Because I know I have a serious heart disease, it has been fixed, but we never know, what is around the corner."

Indeed very insightful at his age. I guess it is his eastern and Zoroastrian upbringing.

We discussed many other issues, his university life and experience in the west, which is different from that of Teheran, had been enlightening to me.

Mr. Bruno, when I saw him first he came with a walker, then from walker he graduated to crutches. He had a personal trainer for certain period of time and an attendant came with him, when his wife or daughter could not accompany him to the rehab center. I saw him and passed by him and regularly greeted him by hand gesture. He also returned my courtesy. After a couple of months I saw him walking on to the track with his crutches. He was having private physiotherapy and exercise by a trainer first and then he will walk with crutches on the track, always with one attendant with him. I frequently walked with him, at other time behind him and most of the time passed by him. We continued to greet with hand gestures.

One day I gathered courage and said good morning to him, so he did that to me also. I said quietly, "How is your day today so far?" He was walking with his crutches with one helper following. "So far, so good," he said, "how about you?" "Slow but steady," I said. "I am nearly 6 months into my rehab program, since my heart surgery, every day is a better day, progress is slow but progress indeed," I said.

"It is just over one and a half years since I was involved in a car crash. My pelvic bone was nearly smashed. I was told I had no chance of surviving with the amount of internal damage and bleeding."

Slowly, walk by walk, pause after pause, Mr. Bruno, told me the story of his life with enthusiasm and asked me several questions, expecting me to give some answer or clues. He was more enthusiastic and at ease, as he found out that I am also recovering like him, and happened to be a doctor.

He owns one of the large car dealerships in the city. Just a cruel mockery of life, a man who has taken care of cars all his life is betrayed by a car, almost lost his life or was going to be bed bound for ever. Unless the surgeons took utmost care of him, and pick on the shattered bones one or two at a time, like fitting them in a jigsaw puzzle. Then he said his bladder had problem could not control, having recurrent infection and fever. On top of these he was paralyzed from the waist downwards. Gradually the pelvic bone was fixed, bladder control was slowly recovering. The last issue is paralysis of my legs. Docs and Surgeons here did more than ten surgical procedures in just over a year. "I needed some sort of surgery in my back for my paralyzed legs, for which they sent me to Mayo Clinic. It was done after I arrived apparently with the help of an operating MRI. I returned back on the fourth day. I started to gain some sensation and strength. That was the quickest and easiest surgery I had, very little scarring and the results I started to get almost instantaneous. Of course, I had resigned to the idea, that I will be paralyzed for the rest of my life, will be wheelchair bound for ever. I kept thinking about Stephen Hawking, the super-genius, who could survey the universe from his wheelchair; why could I not run my car sales business or for that matter any business from my wheelchair? Particularly the last four months have been a huge difference. The exercises, the mild electric shock treatment to improve my strength, have been beyond my wildest expectations."

"I can believe that," I said. "I remember you coming in a wheelchair, then with a walker and now graduated to the crutches. Very soon you will be able to walk without them."

"You know," Mr. Bruno said, "it looks like I will be able to do away with the crutches and be on my two own feet. I am sure it will happen soon, of course God willing."

When he described what started his wretched life about couple of years ago, he seems to have won over all the obstacles to find himself for a fresh start again. Interestingly, despite the awful ordeal he had to go through in his life, the accident, multiple surgeries, urinary and bowel incontinence, paralysis and importantly, pain, discomfort and distress that came with it, he did not seem to despair, always looking for progress and a slightly better tomorrow. Never angry with his doctors or with the system with a firm conviction that whatever is being done should work, will work, just he needed to help by accepting and cooperating with all that is being done for him. So understand, accept and cooperate, has been his strength to recovery. That was a lesson for me from the other side of the table.

I found Mr. O'Brian a very interesting fellow. He has been a steady walking mate at the tracks. He appears to be a gentleman in his late sixties, looked well; I guessed he is a regular health watcher. We said hi to each other but never had any chance to speak to him. Once just after my routine exercises, I went to the cafeteria perhaps for some drink, even plain cool still water would do. I saw Mr. O'Brian sitting in the lounge, reading a newspaper. I grabbed my glass of cold water and headed towards the lounge. I said hello to him and extended my hand. Initially he was hesitant, but after couple of seconds he did extend his hand and shook with me. Mr. O'Brian offered me a seat to share his table.

I introduced myself as someone who is recovering from a major cardiac surgery which was done just over six months ago. I have gotten over the discomfort of surgery, but the side effects from the medications I have to take are a big challenge. But the gain after surgery is worth the pain and a small price to pay with the discomfort and side effect of medications. I mentioned some of my side effects.

He was happy to hear and said, "I had my surgery about 2 years ago, and I still have to take several medications. I have gotten used to some and some have not gotten used to me as yet." We both laughed aloud.

Then Mr. O'Brian introduced himself. He is apparently the president of a large insurance company's regional office in the city. He started with the company as a junior accounts clerk after he emigrated from Ireland. Over the years, with determination and hard work, he became an accounts officer, then an accountant, deputy branch manager, branch manager, regional manager and he had been the regional President for the last six years. There were several steps to cover, several huddles to cross, ups and down here and there. At the age of 59 he became the president of the regional operation of the company. He enjoyed his life, so far. His daughter was married and lived in LA. Two sons were grown up, but one of them was still at the university.

After that over the next few months we sat, chatted had coffee, and discussed our various predicaments. Most conversations ended with a happy note.

He said about a year ago, he started to have chest pain, giddiness and occasional shortness of breath. Before this he had been a picture of health, exercised regularly, did not smoke, occasional Guinness, no hard alcohol, no recreational drugs. He was checked regularly by his family physician. He was not diabetic nor had high blood pressure. He was essentially free from risk to have a heart attack. I was reasonably certain it had nothing to do with the heart.

But unfortunately that was not to be the case. Indeed, the cardiologist after several tests did confirm that my symptoms are due to mild lack of oxygen in my heart muscle, which in medical term is "Angina Pectoris". The news was unpleasant, but we can't avoid the reality.

So my regular visit to Dr. York's chambers and periodic tests continued. In the interim, I was told apparently my blood pressure was getting high, but could be controlled on medication. Life went on.

One morning I went to my office and apparently asked for a glass of hot water. That is not normally what I do. I have a cup of strong coffee. Quickly I go through the emails selected by the secretaries. Then I sit down for morning briefing with senior members of the staff. It never lasts for more than an hour, so that the officers are back to their offices by 9.30 a.m. sharp.

As I finished the briefing one of the parking attendants was waiting outside. She spoke to one of the secretaries and quickly came in and asked for my car key. I was surprised, "What happened? I asked. She was hesitant to answer, but eventually said that perhaps I was in a rush, or I was thinking of some complex problem or perhaps there was not enough light in the parking lot. "You parked your car on the pedestrian crossing." I could not believe what I was hearing. I did not want to make matters any worse. I gave her the key. The attendant parked the car in my designated place. I could not think why it happened? Was it a transient amnesia? This could be an effect of high blood pressure, an early sign of a stroke or a heart attack? I have been catching up with all sorts of popular papers on heart diseases.

The next day I spoke to my GP. He asked me to come down for him to check me up and put me on some kind of medication. My blood pressure was high. He put me on "baby aspirin tablets and sent for some blood tests. He asked me to take a few days off. I thought that would be counterproductive.

Next morning, I went to work and asked for my coffee as usual, usually within half an hour I call for the morning briefing. After one hour, since I did not call, my PA knocked at the door, did not get any response came inside and found me half on the floor, half on the chair. There were CPR-trained staff on every floor. One of them got ready for CPR, but I was breathing and burbling unintelligible sounds. The ambulance was there in five minutes. Fortunately heart hospital was just 10 minutes' drive. Within 15 minutes I was in the ICU.

When I gained consciousness, I saw my wife and two sons standing beside my bed with anxious and grim faces. By that time I was quite awake and asked them what happened and why I was here in the hospital. Then the head nurse gave me the full story that was given to the hospital from my staff members, who were present at that time.

Around 12 noon, the consultant from ICU and the cardiologist came together and explained to me that we just escaped a heart attack. I needed to be in the hospital until they made a diagnosis and worked out a plan of action. After two days of tests and bloodletting, special x-rays and scans, the cardiologist came with the cardiothoracic surgeon. They did not waste much time, but discussed, explained, drew pictures and said that I have quite a few blocked arteries in the heart and I need bypass surgery. Balloons or stenting will not do. Within two days I had four bypasses.

I did get better; my entire family was around me. I am a lot more stable now, but my mind is never free of the possibility of the next attack. What will happen to my family? I know they will not be starving, but there will be a big empty space at home in every activity. My young son is still at the university. There are still a couple of years before he finishes his degree. Then the career path—I have been quite involved if and when they needed any assistance. Who will give them the advice? Who will protect them from the social ills? My older son is not up to take up my role. He has a good job. He is doing well. He has to think and invest his time for career development. He needs to think of having his own family. My daughter is well settled in LA with her husband. With two little kids, she has a handful. One does not know which way life might take a turn. If she needs help I will not be there. I have never been away from these thoughts. At times these are scary and unsettling. I am better. Frequently, I do not have peace of mind; every night I go to bed, not knowing if I will wake up, and if I do, in what shape.

I am sure Mr. O'Brian has plenty to worry, but he can plan ahead for the best possible route to tackle each of them separately or in groups. A successful man, well established in life yet his worries after his heart attacks and death are as grave as anybody else, with emphasis on issues that apply specifically to him.

One day I was waiting to pick up my prescription at the local pharmacy. There were quite a few people waiting. A lady came in; I thought I recognized her face from somewhere. As she reported to the pharmacy, the lady came to the waiting area and said hello to me. I gave up my seat and asked her to sit down. How my exercise and rehab program is coming along? Then I realize, she knows me from my rehab program. In fact she was also in my group for training. I have seen her in seminars. She always looks at me with a smile. I felt she must know me from somewhere other than the rehab.

I also smiled back at her.

I said, "If you are coming to the rehab center, perhaps we could sit for a little while and talk. I would love that. By 11 a.m., I am done with my exercises. Perhaps after that we can talk and learn from each other."

As she said, she was sitting and waiting for her drink and wondering whether to wait for me. She was happy to see me and requested that I sit.

Of course doctors are human beings; they have the right to be sick. But it felt "not right" that you got sick. Then she said perhaps it is unlikely that you will remember me. You treated my dad, who had lung cancer at the cancer center. I used to come with my dad daily during the course of his radiotherapy. He got better. It is difficult to remember faces so many years down the road. But I do remember well, in spite of the age, illnesses, anxiety, stress of life and actually changing effects of the air, sun, shower and the changing environment, do lot to change our body and mind. There are significant physical changes in both you and me and unless we reintroduce ourselves, it would be anybody's guess who we were. But there was something special about your physical features and movements, I had no difficulty in imagining that it was the doctor who treated my dad 25 years ago.

I honestly said, "It is my fault that I did not speak to you earlier."

"So what brought you here?" she asked. I said, "I had bypass operation about 6 months ago. I am taking the rehab exercise program. I feel much better and fortunately, it has worked for me. I plan to continue with the program." I asked how she was doing.

Then she started to speak. She is now a retired high school principal. Just about five months ago she had acute chest pain and within three days she underwent triple bypass operation. She had a satisfactory recovery. She joined the club to take care of herself. She has only one child, a son, who has a very good job with the government civil service. In the last two years he got two promotions. Unfortunately he is separated from his wife. His wife got this idea that she will be a successful Hollywood actress. She has some acting experience. She speaks well. They have one four-year-old and one 18-month-old child. One morning, she told us she was going to L.A. to audition. That was a year ago.

She left her home, husband and two little beautiful kids without giving any thought. So the grandmother is a virtual parent, filling the gap of both mother and father, since he has to be away often on business. Very difficult. Now that I had to have bypass surgery, I do not think I am giving my best attention to the two little jewels. We had to get a nanny, at least for the time being. The two little ones are denied parental love and care, which I would do as I can, but for the time being my heart goes out to them 24 hours a day, 7 days a week.

I could see tears in the grandma's eyes. How one can be so heartless and uncaring for their babies, who they carried around for nine months and then just drop them like hot potatoes? I wish she thought about these two toddlers. We can buy physical care, but no money can buy parents' care, especially a mother's love. We have gone through various channels to trace her; so has her family. Police, private agents, friends—every effort has failed. Now with my condition, if I had to die, that would be the worst curse on me. I cannot forgive myself to leave two beautiful souls, even at death.

We have on several occasions discussed her own illness, her chances of dying from it, reassurances, and mental support, which she needed badly, more than any amount of physio or rehab therapy.

One day I was at the gym, just getting out, and heard, "Hi! Doc, how are you?" I guess he was addressing me, since there was no one else around. Unknown voice, unknown figure. Big stout, muscular man, calling me Doc. As a matter of courtesy, I greeted him and responded appropriately to his question. He came closer. "I am Gerald; I know you — better, I know of you. Stella the receptionist nurse who introduced you to this facility, who also helped you to the program, just happens to be my cousin. She told me she worked with you before she joined this facility. Her house is also not very far from yours. Anyway she thought it might be a good idea to get to know you." "I am very pleased," said I. "Is there anything I can do for you?" So I invited him for a healthy drink at the cafeteria.

We sat down. I asked him, "What kind of work you do here?" He laughed and said, "Actually I am here to join the rehab program." "What happened?" I asked. I thought he was involved in some accident or physical violence and sustained injuries. I could not have been any further off track, after he told me his story.

He has worked in the Merchant's Navy for more than 10 years. He had a good life, good income, a comfortable home where he, his mother and one little sister live. Most of the time he is on board, sailing to various places on ships carrying all kinds of goods: petroleum, mineral ores, consumer goods, etc. Other than petroleum, his boats did not carry any toxic chemicals.

The life-changing event happened when he got married. Within a space of two years they had two children. His wife was also a receptionist – a secretary's job, quite stable. He not being around, his mother was the caretaker for the babies. It was also difficult for his wife to give up the job and meet the household expenses. So he decided to take a shore job. Since he was a Marine technician – to repair, fix and keep all sorts of boats floating and moving – all the jobs are available on the shores, in Halifax, Montreal, Vancouver, etc. Far away from home. To take a shore job, he needs to relocate and uproot his entire family. That was not impossible, but most disruptive to the rest of the family.

Working in big ships, he learned another trade, bartending, quite well. He thought he could do bartending for a little, while looking for an appropriate job. Bartending in the city center is hard and busy. After two days of apprenticing, he was hired as a bartender with an excellent compensation package. This way at least he was with his family and could see his two little kids daily, and relieve some pressure from his ageing mother. He was happy. His customers were even happier. His employer was content with his performance and felt the investment was better than appropriate.

All was going well.

From a boat repairing man to a cocktail mixing person required a huge change in personality and work habit and building a team. A life of quiet smooth sailing to noisy shaking needed adjustment.

One day, he came to work not feeling well and thought some kind of virus he caught from his ever-changing clients at the bar—a perfectly rational explanation. He took some of his Paracetamol extra-strength caplets. Generally it works. In his business shaking and lifting crates all give muscle and bone aches; as they say, it comes with the territory. Pain killers were his most trusted friend.

He still did not feel well. That is all he remembers. When he woke up he realized that he was at the Emergency ward. His wife and sister were outside, waiting for him to wake up. They came in; both were trying to smile. He asked for his mother and children. They were OK. An aunty from next door was with them.

He could not believe what happened. In a just a few seconds his world changed. He did not know which direction life would take him.

He was moved to the ward. There he met the cardiology specialist who said that he had had a minor heart attack. Then with the ward sister and some other specialists, tried to explain what had happened. They would take some more tests over the next few days, then decide the best option for treatment. I was listening, but nothing registered in my conscious mind. I said yes to every question they asked.

In the next two days, X-rays, scans, blood tests, heart tests—all were done at a speed of lightning.

Then at a meeting with my family, the doctors and specialists described the results of all the tests. The conclusion was to go for bypass surgery within the next six to twelve weeks. Other options may not be as good; since I am young and otherwise healthy, the chance of recovery from bypass may be better than the alternatives. They wanted a stable and long term recovery. So about six weeks ago, I had the surgery. I recovered well and now I am at the rehab center for my post-operative recovery program.

What I do not understand is that I had no warning signs, no risk factors to have a heart attack at my age. I wonder if I could have suspected early. I do not know what to suspect, how to suspect. I never had any chest pain or shortness of breath; I have no high blood pressure, and I am not diabetic. I do not have any family history of heart disease. My mother is still alive and well. Dad was much older. As far as we know he died of age and natural causes.

I will do whatever is needed to stay healthy and prevent another attack. If I die, I am dead, but what will happen to my family, my two little kids, my mom? How will the kids grow up without a dad? Of course my wife can marry again, but I will still worry about how the new husband will treat my kids. At times I choke when I think of these.

"Gerald," said I, "if you want to stay healthy and continue to look after your family, remember you are not dead; you are as alive as your next door neighbor, a stock car racing champion. Just plan ahead, as you think and as the doctors and other health care personnel are advising you."

"You know that you are going to get better, and thinking of a full productive life ahead maybe next time. We ponder on this life alone."

The other concern is, I do not want to be a bartender forever. I have skills of fixing ships, boats, and small aircraft. That is what I want to do. But with my sickness, I am sure my employability will be affected. Although the employers will never mention my heart condition, they will find hundred and one reasons to deny me the jobs what I do best."

"Opportunities will come; just keep looking and keep thinking of what will make you happy. You may be good at one craft, but the work environment and people you will be working with may be different. Unless you own your own business that makes you happy."

"You are right, Doc. I can't give up. I must be better at something than what I am good at."

I had not met him for nearly a year when I was "mall walking" with another friend. I heard someone from the back say, Good morning, Doc!" I looked back. It was Gerald. He looked well. We were just about to sit for our morning coffee, so I invited him to join us. He agreed.

He chatted on our "rehab days" his family, how fast the kids are growing, his wife is still working and his mother is still going strong. Then he said, they started their own landscaping business, just about eight months ago. We are a Mennonite clan, so there is no shortage of help. Business has grown so much that my wife is thinking of quitting her job. Anyway, we will take it slow. I still fix all the machineries we use. I remember, Doc, you said one never knows that one may be better at doing things than what he thinks he is good at."

I congratulated him for finding the right spot in life, at least for the time being, wished him well and we departed.

CHAPTER 28: The Epilogue

Why did I write this book? It was very difficult to retrace, recollect various events that took place leading to my heart operation, then nine months of fast recovery and following nine years of slow to very slow recovery. I believe that I am still recovering. The pace is slow but the process is still ongoing. How I nurtured ten years of memory so vividly, at times I felt events are still happening or just finished.

So why did I write this book? It was the medical student at Ross University who asked me one day how he could be a good doctor like me. My answer was quite clear and focused. I said to take his shoes off and wear those of his patients. He is the one who ignited the fire in my mind to put into writing my ten years of experience as a recovering patient after a major and complicated heart operation. I asked him to wear the patient's shoes to understand the patient better. Here, I am already wearing the patient's shoes. I know how it feels; I know every feeling is a learning experience. I thought this is my opportunity to express to the medical community and rest of the world how I felt as a patient and what I can teach them from my personal experience and feelings from this heart operation, what the rest of the healthy world especially other healthy doctors, medical students, nurses, etc. can learn, what their patients might have felt, or the ones to come in future.

The focus here is empathy. Empathy is a feeling when a doc or another health care worker feels exactly like the way patient is feeling, by exchanging shoes. This is a semantic, but says exactly what it means to convey the message. Empathy is a mental phenomenon which makes one individual feel another individual's distress as one's own. Like, love, affection, kindness — these are all mental phenomena, beyond any physical measurement or perceived abstract scale. Pain measurement scales are a perfect example. We have tried to measure pain by using various scales, measurement and cross-measurements. This is what the patient perceives, what the patient feels: on the scale of one to ten what does he feels that is his own feeling? There is no uniformity of perception or of expression. How do we react to the scale? Pain — we use it to select pain killers. But it is the feeling that eludes us.

Of all the symptoms of distress or discomfort human beings present with, "Pain" is the most common and distressing of all symptoms. It can be called the "King" of symptoms. Pain may have a single focal origin to a multi-faceted, multi-systemic origin, but presenting in one particular site. Pain as a manifestation of any disease or as an indicator of unknown cause has been extensively studied and empirically measured and the measurement process adopted in clinical practice. There are several pain measurement scales. All these measurements are generally subjective and based on patient's expression; by giving a number we feel that we are making it objective. As clinicians we have generally no real feeling, when a patient says, "At present my pain score is 8 out of 10." We understand that he has lots of pain, which makes us believe that the patient needs intervention. Our intervention may work in one patient but fail to deliver the same effect to another with same level pain score.

It is something like when your friend visits the Tower of Samarkand and describes that it is slightly shorter than the Eiffel Tower in Paris. It means something to you. You can visualize the height of the Tower of Samarkand. On the other hand, when a resident reports to you that Mrs. "X's" pain is 7 today and Mr. "Y's" pain score is also 7, that does not mean much to me about their pain level, just that it is high. How do they compare to each other for making a management decision? You need to know lot more.

So where is the catch? Pain has multiple provocateurs, i.e., physical, psychological, social, psycho-social, etc. Each of these factors does act independently, yet all lead to a common malady called pain. To be rid of pain completely we need to perceive and tease out all the factors and deal with them individually to achieve our objective, which is getting rid of pain. Dealing with one, the result is inadequate control of the symptoms, leading to dissatisfaction, frustration and continuing distress. Just listening to a pain score or even progressive scores does not reveal the entire story so it remains in the "unfinished" or "to be continued" phase forever, not a satisfactory situation for the patient or the doctor. One needs to go deep into the patient's mind and not just the body. A one-time interview is not enough.

No matter how skillful one is in history and physical examinations, the practice has to be repeated, with an objective to understanding the patient better and treating toward a cure. So multiple interactions with the patient are needed over a period of time for the doctor to learn about the patient and for the patient to gain trust for the doctor. This two-way road needs to be nurtured rather than discouraged on the pretext of emotional involvement, leading to physician burnout. This is a very important issue I intend to expound later.

Since my surgery, any patient I saw, irrespective of my discipline or someone else's, always tried to tie with my feelings while I was a patient.

Even as a patient, the day I actually got sick when I was being routed through the emergency department to the ward, I saw scores of people waiting. Some of them were patients, and others were perhaps accompanied a relative or a friend. Looking at each individual's face, I felt like jumping out of my wheelchair and running to the doctors and nurses to come out and help the people who are in agony. My chest pain and shortness of breath is better, but the memory is fresh and vivid. I asked myself why we can't do the same for these people in distress. That was not a pipe dream; the desire was aroused from my personal sufferings. During the entire course of my surgery, post-operative recovery, rehabilitation, followed by back to work, by design or by accident, the memory of all good and bad times were saved in my brain.

Starting from multiple venipunctures for blood sample, and shaving the whole body on the morning of surgery felt like being a sacrificial creature. My mind indeed went blank of all desire, needs and feelings. A very strange feeling, when I try to recover the same feeling from my deep inner mind. It is the way all the events are so well preserved, even my wildest imagination—they are just linked together. Strike one event, the whole lots of events hidden in the memory come up and sing or cry at the same tune like a grand philharmonic. It is same most of the time. A single string of memory sparks hundreds and then thousands. At times it is a mind-boggling plethora of messages and information. They were all there. Just timing, the right call, and the desire are needed to flood one into a state of empathy to understand and help someone in need.

It is because that I at one time went through the same route memories made me more susceptible to recollect, when a recollection was needed to empathize with another fellow human being who is suffering.

But for someone who does not have the real exposure to "self-injury and distress", there will be no memory to support when he is faced with sickness and suffering. How he can be motivated to be empathetic?

Single tool: Educate

My take is we learn better by repetition. Repetition may not translate into better understanding. By speaking to colleagues, residents and fellows, junior medical doctors, medical students, nurses and other health care workers, by lectures, by mentors are all "one-time" efforts. The impact factor may be so tiny that it may be barely measurable, but the retention factor after one month may be "Zero". It is not practical to repeat classes and seminars, which are essential to make a permanent impact for practice and retention and in their turn be mentors for the next generation. As a substitute for repetition, I documented in my "autobiographical memoir" (as much as I could remember), every interaction with fellow patients, treating doctors, residents, nurses, students, radiologists, other specialists. Most importantly the education to myself by recollecting the events and human interaction, to give my experience to others by preserving this in a document which may be used again and again for perceptive education.

This is one way to mentor the "unempathetic to be empathetic".

Observing anyone in distress due to illness or "in health" made me think of the time when I was on the same route. Because I trod the same path some time in my life, it was easy to connect and feel empathetic when someone is in distress.

Aside from being a patient, I was closer, much closer to people who were sick and needed help, than the doctors and nurses. I could not only watch them physically, but also I could be closer to their mind and soul.

I spoke to patients in the wards, my fellow ward mates. When they realized that I was a doctor, some of them were really surprised at doctor being sick, in the hospital, on a hospital bed, not wearing a white lab coat, with several entourages with the big ones. Eventually we got to talk about our illness, possible treatments, our jobs, our families, some personal concerns, worries and anxieties. I was able to learn more about the patient and got to know them better than had I been in my white coat sitting opposite the table. I certainly did not feel in clinical practice I would be burnt out had I had to speak to the patients at this level of intimacy.

I gave only a few examples of my intimate encounters with several people during my recovery and rehabilitation time, with whom I developed an intimate quasi-professional relation, which may have been their own physician resulted in perhaps better and satisfying outcome of their illness. They may have the relation already, which is just as good as can be. They may want to speak to another person whom they can trust with emotional exposure, especially the high school principal, who had a bypass and was looking after two toddlers, without a mother. Her anguish was heart-wrenching. I was sorry to hear her story, but I feel better that she was somehow consoled by speaking to me. It did take several months of association being a fellow rehabilitator, before she was able to confide in me her real anxiety. Now she knows aside from the medication, exercises, dietary modifications, change in lifestyle, she has another, but perhaps the best, her Doctor-friend with a wide shoulder.

Thousands of years of common wisdom and words from great men and men of letters taught us that in illness, human contact, patient–physician contact, plays an important role in the ultimate outcome of treatment. In traditional medical training it is well appreciated that communication with the patient at every level is a part of medical education. Yet changing cultures, changing priorities and pressure from management has significantly eroded the well-meaning training on patient interview and communication skill given during the four-year education course. Although the curriculum, the teachers, and the program still exist, continuing practice, continuing education and continuing self-assessment are not priorities. Understandably, curricular time, faculty, space for introducing or reinforcing the education and training are sadly missing, replaced by technology, equipment, machineries and electronics used for teaching and teaching aids replacing humans.

Over the millennia great men, great minds, great thinkers, great traditions, like in Judaism, Hinduism, Christianity, Islam, Christ, Confucius, Buddha, Hippocrates, Einstein, Dalai Lama, all had the same advice for humanity: to serve another, to heal another, to understand and care for them, live their lives . For all, especially for the physicians, communicate with heart more than mind with the unfortunate ones, those have fallen ill and are suffering.

We all understand that physicians need to communicate well, better than ever. Social changes, changes in jobs, highly competitive environment, small nuclear families, almost disappearing family support especially in industrialized countries— physical sicknesses are compounded by overbearing psycho-social elements. Unfortunately these psycho-social components are not easily discernable and take much time for the physicians to master, without tackling these issues, healing remains half baked. Neither the doctor nor the patient returns home satisfied.

On the other hand physicians must invest time to understand the patient through both empathy and communication in such a way both the patient and his doctor understands each other clearly. The fallout from this is enormous, maybe even more than the therapeutic interventions. This will make both the patient and physician satisfied. By speaking to the doctor for as long as needed, the patient's faith and trust in the system certainly is enforced. The trust and faith motivates the patient to follow instructions rigidly. With this air of cooperation and mutual faith and respect, the feared "physician burnout" may be reduced significantly, if not completely at one time.

I applaud the act of a group of Canadian physicians in Ontario, who opted to spend more time speaking to their patients heart to heart, looking away from the computer monitor, seeing fewer patients, sacrificing their income and at the end of the day going home much happier than when they spent their half an hour allocated time staring at the computer screen and trying to assimilate tons of data thrown at them from the HER (Electronic Health Record). It is fairly clear now if there is such thing called "physician burnout" it is certainly not due to spending extra time with their patient, but the volume of information overload from various sources including the EHR, the reams of paperwork needed to be done to comply with regulation, pressure from being sued, is one of the main cause of physician burnout in the industrialized countries. In developing countries the stress on physicians leading to perceived burnout is simply, they can't do enough for their patients, what their counterparts in industrialized countries can do. They face this therapeutic vacuum, technological deficit, lack of properly trained health care workers, huge number of patients, day in and day out and experience frustration- led "burnout". The constant barrage of television news advertisements generated in the industrialized countries about advancing technology and how people into developed countries are benefiting puts 80% of human race in an intellectual vacuum and further despair at being "have-nots" and communities of limited or no resources. These ads and news bulletins are specially focused for countries with limited resources to put them into a further state of despondency.

On the other hand, in the developing world they have much better opportunity to satisfy patient's psycho-social needs; with a living social support, perhaps the pressure on the doctors for providing psycho-social therapeutic intervention is less. However, whether the patient is in the developed world or developing countries, every patient, wants to hear from their doctor, wants to speak to their doctors on whatever they want to speak on, would like intimate interaction.

Technology has been a boon to the health care system. It has helped the doctors to stay up to date and the patients to keep informed about their illness; they can anticipate their options and choices. A well-informed patient helps the doctor to reduce the time spent delivering their care. On the other hand, a misinformed patient can be a burden to a physician in the line of his work. The huge amount of information available on the Internet may be informative to a trained mind and diesinformative to an untrained mind. The pressure on the physician is just the same. This, as we can imagine, can work both in favor and against. It is a huge task for physicians to disengage their patients from internet engineered misinformation and reeducate them with proper perspective.

Moreover the blessed one's who are able to avail the force of modern technology are mostly in the industrialized countries that constitute only 20% of the world's population. How much benefit can the American uninsured population utilize for their health from digital communication for physician-patient relationship? There are just over 27 million uninsured people under the age of 65 in USA who do not have access to digital communication to assist them in communicating with their physicians.

So optimism about digital communication improving doctor-patient relation still uncertain in developed countries and it is untenable for the remaining 80% of the world population. There has been some effort to make inroads with digitalization for health care, but the impact is infinitesimal compared to the population and their need.

Education, literacy, computer competence and access to computer, and energy supply are huge problems that need to be tackled, before we jump into the vast "ocean of unknown" in digitalizing health care in for the world's 4.5 billion people. If successful its impact will be unimaginable.

Moreover most people love to speak to their doctors face to face, so for the doctors to communicate better and more effectively, empathetically with a sincere human touch, they will obtain a better outcome, except for few digitally hypnotized ones. Unfortunately or fortunately this is "The State of the Art" for health care-digitalization at present point in time.

I would like to quote Michael Weiner & Paul Bionic (2017): that "Smart IT must accommodate, preserve and uplift interpersonal relationships in health care." Nothing can be truer and more impressive than this.

To improve physician–patient interpersonal communication, even on the part of physicians to realize that this is an important function, we need to have the sense of "empathy". How does one get this "Sense"? Like any "Sense", either you have it, you are born with it or the socio-cultural impact during the course of growing up imposes it on you slowly but surely in a sustainable fashion.

As the strength of a physician's ability to communicate proliferates, thus grows the physician–patient relationship, which is dependent on empathy learned at home as a child, in pre-school, schools, universities and the professional institutes. Psychological, neurobiological and functional MRIs all suggests that human beings are born with some inherited ability of "empathy". If that is true, ability to empathize as adults varies enormously, most likely due to environmental factors, family environment, education, socio-economic conditions, etc.

To have a successful and happy life, we need to be empathetic toward our fellow human beings, for that matter, all that is in our working environment, particularly, physicians and other health care workers need to have a deep sense of empathy. If it is lacking, can we educate ourselves to "regain and expand" our "inherited bit of empathy" if it does exist or motivate ourselves to be empathetic being mentored and trained. In other words can we teach physicians to be empathetic in practice and life in general? The assumption with the aid of "fMRI" is that certain parts of brain are responsible for generation, retention and enhancing the feeling of empathy.

A growing lack of empathy among the medical students, physicians and other health care workers is noticeable, particularly with the exponential rise of medical litigation and immoral and unprofessional acts by physicians. The trend is true for both developed and developing   countries. These need not be.

There are growing numbers of medical educators, deans, and curriculum directors, who are indeed seriously concerned and creating various curricular programs to teach "Empathy" to medical students. The time-honored perception is that one is likely to forget most what is taught, unless that is practiced or used regularly as a part of living. Can empathy be taught? Yes, to get grades on an examination, but hardly to be useful for changing attitudes toward patients or other human beings for that matter, to embed "empathy" in one's mind from an educator's point of view. Courses, lectures, handouts or even methodically teaching how to communicate with patients, the impressions are short-lasting and fade away with time. The reasons are multifaceted. In some, even without their knowledge, the "taught empathy" is tossed out of life, if it is not helping to create wealth. If wealth is created by seeing three patients in one hour without "Empathy", to them it is more desirable than being empathetic, being communicative, spending one hour for one patient's satisfaction, trust and absolute adherence to advice given by the doctor, but stay poor and less wealthy. There is constant social pressure, economic commitments, and bombardment from the industry in the name of innovation, jump into new, poorly tried, barely established practices. Eventually the pressure is on physicians, which severely cost their sense of empathy for their patients.

Education has to take the main role. The classical way of teaching empathy to medical students has essentially been a failure in the long run.

The approach taken by Weill Cornell School of medicine in New York seems to address the issue from the grassroots level till the end. Development of a sense of empathy should start at home even before going to school. So early exposure to being "empathetic" to patients starts in Cornell Curricula from the first day of the first year of medical school till they graduate as MDs. "The goal is to produce doctors who are highly proficient in both scientific and humanistic aspects of medical practice, so they remain focused on treating the whole person, not just the outward signs of their diseases," says Gotto & Glimcher, past and present deans. Weill Cornell has also developed several initiatives for physicians and the principle have been adopted for nursing and other health care workers with some long lasting positive impact. This global patient-physician relation is otherwise defined as clinical empathy.

It is interesting that not the organized curricula, but rather prolonged association with the patient, is the key factor for developing and sustaining an empathetic physician. The time-honored teaching and concept, that "a close patient-provider relationship threatens objectivity, therefore a social distance is expected to ensure professionalism" (Kadushin, 1962). This principle in medical education is known as clinical detachment.

The physician's factor of clinical detachment deals with the emotional impact of death and dying, avoidance of mistakes, diagnostic and prognostic uncertainties, emotional inhibition and subjugation, conceptual rationalization and at times witty jokes used for communicating objectively with patients, on the principle of clinical detachment. If our objective is detachment, no matter what method we use, what caricature we perform, it will be hard to obtain patient's faith, understanding and loyalty, thus hampering the patient–physician relationship, which we think is an absolute necessity in optimizing health care. The notion is that an emotionally engaged physician leads to poor judgment by the physician. Interestingly, several studies and observations showed just the opposite. This dictum needs to be re-conceptualized before we hand it over to medical students and physicians.

This is my autobiographical memoir, which was inspired by one of my students asking how he could be a good doctor like me. My reply was to exchange shoes with the patient and only then will you be a good doctor on your own and need no help from anyone else; the help will come from your inside, your sense of empathy, as you will intimately feel what the patient is feeling, how the patient is feeling. No one else but you would have that knowledge and the feeling and be the best doctor for him.

Months after I thought that, in fact I was a patient myself and went through the ordeal of a "triple bypass"; the "Shoe" I was wearing then, even ten years down the road I am still wearing now, being followed up by my GP and Cardiologist.

To explain or educate someone, I need not slip my foot into anyone's shoe. I am indeed the "shoe". My memories are still intact. I can pull the events, my feelings of the entire treatment till today, out not only from my brain, but also from my heart, and they might inspire and generate a sense of empathy in colleagues, students, and other health care workers. Also, this may be a preparatory note to the general public to understand and feel the process from the heart, since in the modern day and age we all are at risk of heart attack and cardiac surgery.

This book intimately recalls all events, all feelings from the time of surgery till now, and attempts particularly to encourage medical students, physicians and healthcare workers to experience something from some other's point of view, some others' pain and distress, yet with a sensation of "my body over there". Thus, I expect one to get immersed into a clinical situation, so that the individual can deeply understand and anticipate the patient's feeling with "empathy".

Thus this autobiographical memoir will not only encourage readers but also engage them to be empathetic toward their patients, distressed friends, relatives, and the neighbor who seeks advice or maybe a broad shoulder to lean on a time of desperation.

There is psychometric and neurobiological experimental evidence which indicates that with deep and entrenched empathetic feeling, the process further extends into phenomenon of "prospection", which allows practitioners to predict the future, and generally emanates from (autobiographical) memory. In this case by developing the sense of "empathy", it may be possible to prospectively determine the future to come. Evidence from "fMRI" suggested by Robert Eres (2015) is that areas of brain — insula, cingulate cortex, dorsomedial prefrontal cortex — which are involved in empathy, shares significant functional aspects of human prospection. Further studies extended these areas to be functionally active in mental time travel (MTT). The scientific growth of Neuro-biology has been phenomenal. Yet we are scratching the surface only.

It is intended that this book will stimulate growth and sustenance of the feeling and incorporation of "empathy" into not only medical practice, but also all human contacts, and from there to develop the sense of prospection, for long term association with patients and other fellow human beings, for faster and more comprehensive healing, with significantly less cost and avoidance of the hazards of various therapeutic interventions and less litigation. With the rest of the society, happy association, and long term friendships and lives will be fulfilled.

Fast conceptual development and changes in medical science and the practice of Medicine, IT and Technology's participation in medical practice—impact has been both a blessing and a curse at the same time. Physician burnout due to data and paperwork overload, reduced or insignificant patient-doctors contact is on the wrong side. But well-informed patients, info gathered from IT, from various websites are making the public informed—and sometimes dis-informed. This makes life easy and difficult at the same time, when the physicians have to spend longer to fend off misinformation and misconceptions gathered by patients. Info and printed words are frequently trusted more by patients than doctors with years of training and experience. This situation is unhelpful and detrimental for making appropriate decisions.

Technology by every 24-hour innovations is pushing the cost of treatment high. Stress on funding and financing bodies. Keeping up with technical and technological advances is also putting stress on the system. But it is happening; health care institutions are finding it difficult to match. But it is being matched, at a cost of reduced patient care.

In this context I can't overlook the comments made by Peter Wessel Zapffe as early as 1933: "Life had overshot its target and blown itself apart. A species had been too heavily armed—its genius made it not only all-powerful in the external world, but equally dangerous to its own well-being." Zapffe did not have to wait eighty years to see what is happening now.

However, on the contrary, many conscientious and thoughtful individuals, including Dean Antonio Gotto and Ex-Dean Laurie Glimcher of Weil Cornell at New York believes that "Technology—whether a robot or a DNA sequencer—can provide a lot of information and make our job easier, but there is no substitute for a caring relationship between a physician and a patient."

We have to "keep the patient at the center of everything we do". The first and foremost change we need is to train all physicians with a strong and sustained sense of empathy. Undoubtedly Weil Cornell and few others are headed in the right direction.

Science, technology, and human genius appear to have partnered with industry and a market economy as espoused by worldwide capitalism mostly in industrialized countries, who need to take note of the observation made by Michael Weiner and Paul Biondich (2017): "Smart IT must accommodate, preserve and uplift interpersonal relationships in health care".

Billions of dollars are poured into research by industry for the improvement and safety of humanity.

As it stands now, there is a tug of war going on between technologies, supported by industries on the principle of capitalism with "HUMANISM".

In this war it is obvious that capitalism and a market economy are the big winners. At this point humanism stands no chance against the tsunami of faith in the market economy, as the only savior of mankind.

But millions of good people with good sense, heavy heart, faith, compassion, and empathy will win over this lopsided all-round social disparity, when capitalism will voluntarily relinquish its own burden of conscience. The signs are already there. I am not naming Bill Gates in this context. Education, Harvard, technological success, all happened or could have happened with or without any of the factors made him the world's richest man, but in the end the heavy burden of success made him empathetic to other human beings who are not as lucky as he is.

The result is a huge "off -loading" of his capitalistic success to be shared by others. Bill Gates is one but there are many others who are bestowed luck from capitalism, technological innovations and the burgeoning market economy who are searching for the right way to live and to make life better for others. If this sense of sharing came earlier in their lives, many other could have been benefited from their success. The essence is in feeling empathy for others needs to be instilled earlier in life; that is a part education is most likely missing. I can't stress enough that this is no different in the case of doctors or for that matter all human beings.

"The highest realms of thoughts are impossible to reach without first attaining an understanding of compassion."
                                                                - Socrates

Dr. Kamalendu Malaker is a qualified physician from R.G. Kar Medical College at the University of Calcutta, India. He obtained his PhD in cell biology from the Imperial College in London, and trained in Clinical Oncology at the University of Oxford. His training finished at the Royal Post Graduate Medical School at Hammersmith Hospital. Subsequently, he was appointed senior registrar and clinical tutor for the University of London.

Subsequently, Dr. Malaker moved to Canada where he headed the radiation oncology department at Cancer Care Manitoba and at the University of Manitoba in Winnipeg. His work continued as a research officer at the Dana Farber Cancer Center at Harvard University in Boston.

Dr. Malaker's expertise then took him to Libya in North Africa, where he was instrumental in developing radiation oncology services for the country and performed post graduate training in clinical oncology for Libyan Board. He was consulting clinical oncologist for the Government of United Arab Emirate, and then assumed the role of chairman of The Princess Noorah Oncology Center in Jeddah, Saudi Arabia. Dr. Malaker's career tract also included the role of District Medical Officer in Sierra Leon in Sub-Saharan Africa, which impacted deeply in his future life.

Dr. Malaker then headed to the Caribbean where he joined Ross University School of Medicine as a visiting professor of ICM and Oncology. Concurrently, he developed the oncology services unit for the Government of Dominica at Princess Margaret Hospital. In his present capacity, Dr. Malaker also carries the title of Director of

Clinical Oncology at The Cancer Centre Eastern Caribbean in Antigua.

A clinician, researcher, teacher, mentor, writer and director, Dr. Malaker he has left his legacy behind in every place he has worked. He has published more than 100 scientific papers and numerous books; one of which was a best seller for several years. His hobby of writing on travelogue, social issues, human right issues, climate change and many more, has produced more than forty essays and articles over several years. In recent years, he has successfully published popular titles such as "My Personal Health Record ", a manual personal health record compendium, and "The Plasma", a medical thriller.

His current interest is to develop equitable cancer therapy and management in countries with limited resources where eighty percent (80%) of world's population lives. While he continues to write on the human condition, he credits his vision and aspirations to his multi-racial and cross cultural exposure through his work and travels. He still remains an avid global traveler and lives with his wife Baljit in Winnipeg, Canada. They have one daughter and two granddaughters.

32729745R00157

Made in the USA
Columbia, SC
14 November 2018